Big Dick Energy

Big Dick Energy

How to Be Well-Endowed
(with Healthy Male Confidence)

by Matt Murphy

Big Dick Energy: How to Be Well-Endowed (With Healthy Male Confidence) is a work of nonfiction. The events, anecdotes, and experiences described herein are drawn from the author's own life and observations. Names, identifying details, and certain characteristics have been changed to protect the privacy of individuals.

ISBN: 979-8-218-77206-2

For information, permissions, or bulk orders, contact:
MANifestos Media
Mount Plymouth, FL
manifestosmedia@gmail.com

Cover design by Matt Murphy
Edited by Shara Allen

Printed in the United States of America
10 9 8 7 6 5 4 3 2 1

First Edition

Table of Contents

To Shara – For bringing out the best in me.

Introduction

What kind of asshole writes a self-help book?

It takes a special kind of audacity to think you're crushing life so hard you should hand others the roadmap.

Hopefully, he's an honest asshole. You don't need pep talks or smoke blown up your ass; you need truth.

Here's the truth about me, the man writing this self-help book: I'm not a full-time writer. I have a normal job and have been writing in my free time. Lately, I've had more free time than I can afford. Work has been slow. My industry has changed, and I've struggled to adapt while staying true to myself. I'm unsure if I'll make rent by the end of the month.

That is where your self-help author is today. But I've built Big Dick Energy, and I know I'll get through this.

Five years ago, I wouldn't have been able to admit any of that, even to my closest friends.

Why am I telling you this, stranger?

Because truth is the foundation of Big Dick Energy.

Because showing you where I struggle now — not just in the past — proves this isn't some fix-all fantasy.

Because I'm no one special. Just a man who's walked through

the fire and believes honesty is the anchor for respect, resilience, and relationships.

A few weeks ago, I started listening to a bestselling self-help book during a commute. The introduction hooked me. The first chapter hit hard. Then the author added a made-up experience to raise the emotional stakes. In nonfiction, that's a dealbreaker for me.

It's one thing to paint a vivid picture. It's another to color outside the lines of truth to sound profound. A nonfiction author doesn't get to invent emotional fireworks. We all understand the pain of stubbing a toe without needing the scene to include a lightning strike, a flaming shoe, and a bald eagle taking a dump on your head.

I'm making this promise: I won't bullshit you. I'll recount personal anecdotes as honestly as memory allows, without fluff or fireworks, although I'll paraphrase direct quotes as needed without straying from the truth. Names will be changed when necessary to protect others' privacy and keep my ass out of court.

Here's another truth: You can read this book a hundred times and follow all the recommended steps, but you'll still never have your shit together all the time. Sure, you might have sustained periods of stability, but you're one of eight billion people trying to hold your shit together, held down by gravity on a ball of gas spinning a thousand miles an hour as it orbits through infinite space.

We all trip over our own feet, and sometimes life knocks us on our asses.

This book won't give you a perfect life or shield you from life's unpredictable storms, but it will provide you with the tools to rebuild yourself stronger, own your truth without shame, and develop resilient masculine confidence no matter what life throws at you.

I hadn't heard of Big Dick Energy until a twenty-something at a dive bar pointed it out in me. She'd been watching — how I carried myself, how I treated my lady — and said, "That's Big Dick Energy." It hit me because she put a name to something I'd been rebuilding quietly from the rubble after my life fell apart four years earlier.

But I didn't get here easily.

I'd built the tower of my identity on a foundation of ego. When life demolished that tower and left a hole in the earth where I once stood, I reconstructed myself with better materials — healthier habits and mindsets. Now, I stand stronger than ever, grateful for life's brutal lessons, and humble enough to know it can all come crashing down again in a heartbeat.

The mirror shows me I've become a good man, and the people who matter the most to me agree. I've learned to love myself and finally learned to love someone else the right way. Like Andy Dufresne at the end of *The Shawshank Redemption*, I've swum through the mud and shit and come out clean on the other side.

Work issues aside, my life is better than ever. If it turns into a shit-show tomorrow, I've built the confidence and competence to know I'll be back on my feet and pressing forward the next day.

I'm neither a guru nor a scholar. But life has given me a master's degree in getting knocked down and a doctorate in getting back up — rebuilding by facing hard truths, taking accountability, and learning from my mistakes.

I'm not here because I've studied it; I'm here because I've survived it.

This is the book I wish I'd had ten years ago. I don't have all the answers, but I've lived enough hard truths to know which questions matter. If this book helps you, it was worth my time — and, if we're being honest, I hope it's worth a few bucks of yours, too, because inspiration feeds the soul, but it doesn't pay the rent.

Chapter One
What is Big Dick Energy?

Let's start with a truth you probably know but still need to hear: Big Dick Energy (BDE) has nothing to do with your actual dick.

No stretch, supplement, pump, pill, prayer, or PornHub link will give you a lasting, healthy increase in penis size. If that's what you came for, I respect the optimism (and I'd love the link if you find the holy grail). But what we're talking about here isn't physical. It's psychological — maybe even spiritual, if you're into that.

Big Dick Energy is a vibe. A presence. It's calm, grounded confidence that doesn't need to shout or swagger. When a man with BDE walks into a room, he makes eye contact, gives a firm (but not forceful) handshake, and listens more than he talks. He doesn't need to dominate to feel strong or cut others down to stand tall.

You've seen Big Dick Energy in celebrities, from ripped heart-stoppers like Jason Momoa to brilliant nerds like Jeff Goldblum. But you've also seen it in real life: your buddy's laid-back, charismatic dad who somehow owns every room without trying.

And maybe, if you've ever been to a gym, you've witnessed

him: the naked old guy in the locker room.

You know the one.

He's not ripped. He's not rich. He's not the least bit concerned with hiding time and gravity's inescapable effects. He towels off at a leisurely pace — belly hanging, his little buddy peeking through the shrubbery — unfazed by public scrutiny. As much as you try not to look, you do (everyone does). Not out of curiosity but out of awe. How the hell is this guy so comfortable in his own skin?

He has Big Dick Energy.

Not because he's packing heat — he's probably not — but because he gives zero fucks about your judgment. Porn hasn't destroyed his self-image, so he doesn't obsess over being less hung than John Holmes, and he's proud that his little helper has spawned three children who are now grown and in the business of making him grandchildren. He's earned something most men spend their whole lives chasing: a confident peace with himself, flaws and all.

Now, ask yourself this:

Why wait until I'm 70 and saggy to find that kind of self-acceptance? Why not now, while I still have knees that bend and a penis that rises?

The Definition of Big Dick Energy

The term "Big Dick Energy" hit the mainstream when a Twitter user named @iambobswaget Tweeted:

Pete Davidson is the only person I've ever seen with Big Dick Energy.

The Tweet referred to Davidson's ability to land high-status women with a magnetic confidence that didn't come from looks or bravado but from a presence that seemed effortless.

It struck a nerve by putting language to a vibe people had long recognized but never quite named. Suddenly, everyone could point to someone they knew who had it. It's since been adopted into our zeitgeist as an overarching description of a man based on his vibe, not his penis size; it's a calm self-assuredness that doesn't try too hard.

It's not toxic masculinity. I'm not talking about the watered-down definition of "toxic masculinity" used to bash men for having a backbone. I mean the real kind: insecure, violent, chest-beating bullshit that causes real harm.

It's also not the neutered, self-loathing version of masculinity that apologizes for existing. It doesn't flinch at strength, ambition, or the biological instincts that come with being a man. BDE doesn't shrink to make others comfortable or deny its masculine energy to gain approval. It owns who it is with humility, not shame.

You don't have to reject your manhood to be a good man; you just have to wield it responsibly with honesty, confidence, and compassion.

What we're shooting for here is to become a Keanu Reeves: respected, kind, humble, never bragging or overcompensating, and moving through the world like a man with nothing to prove. And if we end up filthy rich like him along the way, all the better.

Big Dick Energy doesn't care what color you are, who you sleep with, where you're from, or even which gender you are. It isn't reserved for any one group. You either earn it through mindset, action, and how you show up in the world — or you don't.

In my corner of the world, the consensus is that I've earned my Big Dick Energy, but it didn't come easy. And it damn sure didn't grow in my pants. It took me forty-five years, two divorces, a health collapse, a soul-stripping public campaign for help, the decimation of my pride, and a long swim through the cesspool of online dating. I had to face hard truths, take accountability, and draw clear boundaries for myself and others. I walked away from a career others envied. When I hit rock bottom, I was a shell of a man, performing masculinity without any of its strength, quietly wishing I wouldn't wake up the next day.

It wasn't until I stopped filtering every thought and action through layers of self-doubt and social expectation that I started becoming the man I truly am.

Confidence isn't something you fake; masculinity isn't something you force. Your status, income, body count, dating app success — even your dick size — doesn't define your worth.

This book is about burning all that bullshit to the ground and building something real in its place:

- Confidence that trades arrogance for humble self-awareness.
- Masculinity that isn't based on dominance.
- A quiet strength that comes from truth, not performance.

It sounds like a tall order, but I'll walk you through every step. By the end of this book, you'll be ready to own your shit.

Big Dick Energy is already in you. Let's dig it out, polish it up, and let it shine. (It's a metaphor. Keep your pants on…for now.)

Let's go.

Chapter Two
The Catalyst

Big Dick Energy isn't just something you find in care-free old men or cool-headed celebrities. It's something you earn in the fire by stepping into situations that test your self-worth and coming out a little wiser, a little tougher, and a lot more real.

For me, one of those fires was online dating.

One Saturday afternoon in 2023, I sat across from a dark-haired middle school principal named Cathy while we picked at our breakfast at a trendy diner in Deland, Florida. In the 18 months since divorcing my second wife, I'd gone on more than a hundred dates from various dating apps. I joked to my friends that I deserved a humanitarian award for feeding half the single women in Central Florida.

I went through the motions, saying the usual right-sounding things to come off like a well-adjusted, confident suitor, but my heart wasn't in it this time. I was bitter that photo filters and high-angle selfies had fooled me — again. Cathy still could've won me over with a great personality, but she was as flavorless as my overpriced omelette.

As we talked, I noticed her eyes fixate on my teeth several times. They were darkening, and a stain had emerged between my front teeth in recent months. Vaping and coffee will do that — once I figure out how to kick those habits, maybe I'll write another self-help book, and you can drop another few bucks into my rent fund.

I was doing well enough on dates to qualify as a middle-aged fuckboy (*piss off, Spell Check*), but I wasn't getting much sustained interest, even from women I'd have passed on a few years earlier. Most treated me like a moped: fun to ride, as long as their friends didn't see them straddling it.

That's dating in the Instagram era, where how you present yourself (and your love interest) online matters more than anything.

When the date ended, Cathy and I traded a mutually apathetic hug and parted ways.

I sat in my car, sulking and unsure why. She did nothing for me; I wasn't attracted to her looks or personality, and I sure as hell wouldn't have wasted good cologne on a second date.

Was I seriously pouting because someone I didn't want also didn't want me?

Was my ego really that fragile?

I'd faced plenty of rejection in my life, but I'd never let it tamp down my optimism — until I tried online dating in my forties.

This wasn't me.

After Cathy pulled away, neither of us knew our date lit a spark that was about to ignite change.

I flipped down the visor and checked my teeth in the mirror. I needed to do something; it'd been years since I smiled freely.

I checked my phone and saw a new match on Facebook Dating. Her name was Laura, a pretty brunette nurse with a nice Florida beach body. I remembered sending her one of those long-shot Likes you throw out just in case the universe is in a good mood.

Her message popped up: "Hey Matt. I'm Laura. Nice to meet you. Have any fun weekend plans?"

A little sunlight cut through the gloom. *Fuck it,* I thought. *What do I have to lose?* I replied: "Nothing planned except dinner with you tonight."

She responded instantly: "LOL, are you serious?"

I threw down the gauntlet. The real me was hitting a home

run or striking out in style.

Me: "Let's do it!"

This wasn't false bravado. I'd spent months playing it safe, swinging for singles. But now, I wasn't afraid of striking out or coming on too strong. The rush of confidence felt surreal and long overdue.

Laura: "I have plans with my daughters tonight. Can we do lunch tomorrow?"

Me: "Whoa. You move fast."

Laura: *laughing emoji*

Me: "If you're up for live music and greasy food, let's meet at Sidewinders tomorrow at noon."

Laura: "I have church until noon. Let's make it 1:30. Here's my number!"

I sat in my car and stared at my phone. *Holy shit! Did that just happen?*

I'd been through the wringer on the dating apps: matching with dozens of women, meeting two or three a week, getting laid plenty, sleeping too little, spending too much money, and dealing with a whole lot of craziness.

How crazy? I'm glad you asked. One woman told me, two sips into my first beer, that she was into watching dog-on-woman porn. (No second beer for me.) All this while I was still trying to say and do the right things to make women like me. But when I finally acted like myself — bold, honest, and a little silly — I scored a date with an attractive woman in under three minutes.

It was my first step down the path to authenticity.

The next day, I met Laura for lunch. We exchanged a hug and sat down to order a couple of beers while scanning the menu.

"They allow smoking out here," I said.

Laura gave me a shy grin. "What makes you think I'm a smoker?"

"The only nurses who skip the smoking question on dating apps are smokers," I laughed.

"You don't mind?"

"Not at all. But who cares what I think? You're a smoker. If that were a dealbreaker for me, you'd know I wasn't the right guy for you."

Laura smiled, leaned across the table, and kissed me. "That would be a shame."

We talked, she smoked, I vaped, and we knocked back our beers while waiting for the food. I stayed unfiltered, swapping nightmare dating stories and half-joking about why she shouldn't date a guy like me.

"We could get to-go boxes, you know," she said. "Want to come back to my place?"

"I'd love to," I said, "but I think we'd enjoy it even more if we waited for date two."

What are you doing, idiot? screamed the man-child inside me who craved validation through sex. *She's hot. You like sex. Don't blow this!*

But this time, the brain between my ears overruled the one between my legs. I was ready for something more.

Laura jolted. "Wow. Okay. That's actually kind of hot. Can we make that second date happen tomorrow?"

"Six o'clock work for you?" I asked. "We'll get Chinese take-out and see where things go."

"That sounds perfect."

What followed was a whirlwind fling with a woman I once thought was out of my league. And it all happened because I ditched the insecurity, gave my fear of rejection a defiant middle finger, took a risk, and showed up as my true self.

The relationship never fully took root. We weren't the right match; Laura was looking for someone whose religious values aligned more closely with hers. (Yes, she invited me back to her place after church, but I wasn't there to judge.) Things faded after a month.

We're each oddly shaped puzzle pieces with unique sockets and slots. If we shape-shift to try fitting in where we don't belong, we'll never connect where — or with whom — we do.

A few days after Laura and I ended things, something clicked. Sure, I was disappointed it didn't work out and dreaded a return to dating apps, but I realized I'd never have landed that date with her, let alone shared the short, exciting romance, if I hadn't led with boldness and authenticity.

Before I jumped back into online dating, I made a decision; this time, the real me was showing up. But I had to put in some work to find that guy first.

My first step was to take a long, honest look in the mirror — not for soul-searching but to see what the world saw when it looked at me.

Back in my twenties, I had a bit of style: frosted tips, snug shirts, a pro-wrestler's fake tan. That guy was long gone. Now? The mirror reflected a low-effort guy with no edge. My torso wardrobe was full of all the 2-for-$25 graphic tees I could fit on my Kohl's card. I laughed and cringed, remembering a three-week side quest a year earlier with a woman named TerriLynn, who ended things because I wore a Cap'n Crunch T-shirt on a date. And I'd gotten so used to hiding my stained teeth, I forgot what it felt like to smile without feeling self-conscious.

I wasn't about to change who I was, but I could tighten up the way I presented myself.

I went to the dentist for a deep clean, and the stains vanished. Then I updated my wardrobe. I bought clothes I'd always wanted to wear but never had the nerve to, worried I'd look like I was trying too hard. How the hell does a guy pick the perfect Hawaiian shirt, anyway?

At 46, I'd like to call it anything but a glow-up, but that's exactly what it was.

This was the Matt Murphy I wanted to see — and the one I wanted the world to meet.

I also stopped saying what I thought people wanted to hear and instead spoke plainly and truthfully. I quit chasing approval and started showing up as myself.

Not everyone loved it; some dates got visibly uncomfortable when I gave them the unfiltered version of myself.

Jennifer, a marketing exec with a great smile, told me over drinks about a time she had lettuce stuck between her teeth during a Zoom meeting. "I was mortified," she said. "What about you? What was your most embarrassing experience?"

I told her about when I accidentally (and loudly) sneeze-farted during a wedding.

Just like that, any romantic interest she might have had in me dried up on the spot.

"You're hilarious," she laughed. "But there's no way I could bring you to my company Christmas party."

Message received, and lesson learned: being real without any filter isn't authenticity but a mask of bluntness and bravado.

In learning to be myself, I overshot the mark and became performative in my realness. When I dialed it back a few notches, I found a rhythm that felt honest but palatable.

That shift set the stage for someone incredible to walk into my life. We'll get to her soon. Trust me: she's worth the wait.

Matt Murphy

Chapter Three
Finding Yourself Amid the Wreckage

There's a scene in every great disaster movie where the main character walks through the wreckage.

Everything's gone to shit.

The world is ablaze.

The Statue of Liberty's head is inevitably sinking to the bottom of the ocean or washed up onto the shore.

And the hero realizes something: the old life is gone.

That moment? It's not the end of the story. It's the beginning of a new chapter.

That's when real confidence is born. Not when life's going smoothly. Not when you're killing it at work, crushing it at the gym, or stacking matches on the dating apps. Confidence rises from personal rubble — bruised and bleeding, embarrassed and emasculated — when you realize you're still standing, still breathing.

I've been there.

Rock Bottom

In 2021, at forty-two, I lived the most difficult year of my life.

My second marriage was a full-blown emotional tornado.

My teenage son had moved a thousand miles away to live with his mom.

Days after my birthday, doctors told me I couldn't work or drive anymore due to a seizure disorder. I saw dozens of doctors and specialists and ended up in the ER more than ten times.

I was forced to leave a dream job. My boss kindly offered to start a GoFundMe campaign, but I declined. My pride didn't want to accept help from anyone. But our wives talked that night, and I woke up the next morning to find the fundraiser had been started, and over ten grand had already been raised. I felt humiliated, convinced that people who once admired me now pitied me. (Later, I'd realize they just fucking *cared* about me.)

Everything I'd worked for, everything I'd built, everything I valued was gone.

My identity was in pieces.

I was over forty, missing my son, stuck beside a partner I loathed, jobless, physically and financially disabled, and emotionally numb.

I quietly prayed to a God I wasn't sure I believed in to let me die in my sleep.

That was rock bottom.

Here's what no one tells you when everything you've built collapses: stripped bare, exposed to your core, you finally meet the real you. Beneath the rubble, there's just you and the truth; you learn who you are and what matters.

In the stillness, you choose the man you want to become and the life you want to live. When there's nothing left — when even the foundation is reduced to ash — that's your moment to turn tragedy into opportunity. To rebuild from the ground up.

Not the version of you trying to prove something.

Not the guy you became to avoid conflict.

Just you: raw, unfiltered, and brutally honest.

Then you stand.

It sucks to go through. But it's enlightening as hell to get through.

The Golden Repair

When I hit rock bottom, I didn't just feel broken — I felt like there was nothing worth repairing. Everything I'd cared about was in pieces, and I didn't know where to start.

Then I learned about the Japanese art of *kintsugi*. It's the practice of repairing shattered pottery with gold-filled lacquer so the cracks aren't hidden, but illuminated. The damage becomes part of the story, a visible reminder of survival.

I kept thinking about that: the idea that what breaks you can become the most beautiful part of you if you're willing to repair it with something valuable.

My gold wasn't literal. It was the truths I faced in therapy, the brutal self-examination I couldn't avoid, the conversations that stripped away every excuse I'd been clinging to.

Big Dick Energy is to men what *kintsugi* is to pottery: a golden repair of your brokenness. Resilient. Honest. Unashamed of the scars that prove you've lived.

When you break — and you will — what will you use to hold yourself together?

(That's a rhetorical question. You'd better use gold, or I'll deny you ever read this book.)

Now, back to our regularly scheduled programming of bad words and good advice.

When my life collapsed, my ego came down with it. I started peeling away its remnants through hard conversations — with myself, and with my therapist, Catalina.

Catalina was a Cuban immigrant who rarely spoke, but when she did — broken English or not — it landed. Every Tuesday morning for a year, I monologued through most of my sessions. Some therapists coddle or overanalyze. Catalina? She called bullshit on my bullshit and pushed me to own my circumstances.

"You're being…how you say? Delusional," she'd say with a

stern look.

No one had ever spoken to me that directly — not friends, not partners, and certainly not myself.

Determined to rebuild stronger, wiser, and better, I swallowed the hard truths. Truth is the binding agent in the BDE lacquer.

My first marriage didn't fall apart because of her affair; that was just the accelerant. It ended because we neglected ourselves — and each other. The second one was doomed from the start because I rushed into it, ignoring more red flags than a Chinese parade along the way. My health broke down because I overextended myself and ignored warning signs. Every disaster had my fingerprints on it.

I let go of blame and took full responsibility for all of it.

I faced my insecurities and fears. Nothing I was afraid of was worse than what I'd already survived.

I learned from my failures.

I forgave others — and myself.

Peace followed.

I was becoming the man I was always meant to be.

My Big Dick Energy was rising.

So was my belief that I could get it right next time.

When You Lose Everything, You Find Yourself

Stripped of everything that mattered, I had no choice but to ask: "Who the hell am I?"

I'm a guy who loves kayaking and country music, John Wayne movies and good books, corny jokes and even cornier '80s music videos. I'm a man who listens attentively, shares openly, and shows up for his friends when it counts. I return my shopping carts and hold doors — not for praise, but because it feels right. But I'd buried that guy beneath layers of ego and image management.

When my carefully curated image toppled, it made room for something real to rise.

Rising After the Fall

Lying under the rubble after your life crumbles, you're only a failure if you stay buried there. You start winning the moment you stand.

It might be too late to save a relationship or a job, but that doesn't mean it's too late to improve yourself so you can do better next time.

You're working toward becoming a man who doesn't measure himself by wins but by who he is when he's losing, who doesn't talk a big game but can stand strong with a quiet presence, and who can handle the pain, face the truth, and come out the other side better without bitterness.

Your Turn: The Three Hardest Moments

Here's a quick practice. Grab a notebook and jot down:
1. The three hardest moments of your life.
2. What each one taught you.
3. How they changed the way you see yourself.

Now look closely at that list. That's your wreckage. That's where the real you is hiding: under the rubble, waiting to rise. That's where you find true confidence.

Confidence isn't thinking that nothing can knock you down. It's knowing you can take a punch and stay in the fight.

The guy who brags he's never lost a fight? He's never had to bleed, recalibrate, and claw his way off the ground. He's never endured that brutal moment when he's taken all he can — and the beating's just getting started. The first time he hits the ground, he crumbles.

I'd rather be the guy who's been dropped ten times — because those are ten times I found the grit to rise, own my mistakes, and come back tougher.

Here's where I began my climb out of the rubble.

Near the end of the worst year of my life, I was cleared to return to work. "You've been misdiagnosed," one neurologist told me. A second one agreed, and I got the green light.

Two weeks later, I was back at work.

Less than two months later, I woke up, looked at my second wife, and said, "I don't want to be your husband anymore. I'm done."

That was the start of my rise. Your journey will look different, but the process is the same. To rise, you have to face what the collapse left behind.

Disaster movies end when the hero rebuilds from the wreckage. In real life, it's the start of a new chapter — hopefully one where you find out you're not the only one who's walked through the fire.

Chapter Four
You're Not as Unique as You Think

So many men are feeling the same things — fear, insecurity, sadness, loss — but we rarely connect with each other on an emotional level. It's like we're all trapped in the same freezing room, waiting to see which poor bastard will admit he's cold first.

Good news: You're not as unique as you think.

You make room for real connection when you let go of the pressure to be one-of-a-kind and the lie that no one else has been through what you have.

One of the fastest ways to kill your confidence is to believe you're alone in your struggles. That no one else knows what it's like to be you, and that your flaws are too weird, your insecurities too embarrassing, your screw-ups too shameful to share. So, you isolate. You pretend. You hide.

But here's the truth: you are not alone.

That stupid thing you've done? Someone else has done it.
Those dark thoughts you've had? Someone else has had them.
The fear you wrestle with? Someone else has already squared

off against it.

That random boner you got with your dog in your lap? You're not the only one, pal.

The moment you understand that, a massive weight lifts off your shoulders. You realize you're human: flawed, not defective. And that's the beginning of real self-acceptance.

We love to romanticize being different. It gives us an out. An excuse to say things like:

"People just don't get me."

"They won't understand what I'm going through. My pain is different."

"I can't make friends. I'm not like them."

That's not truth. That's fear. You worry that if people knew what was really going on inside, they'd walk. So you build walls. You pull away.

But confidence — real, grounded, Big Dick Energy-level confidence — doesn't come from standing apart. It comes from standing with.

Connection Through Common Ground

"She fucking cheated," I told my friend Paul over lunch at a pub in 2018.

He shook his head. "I'm sorry, man. How are you doing?"

"Honestly? I keep picturing myself smashing her slimy, chicken-shit coworker's skull with a claw hammer."

Paul pulled out his wallet.

Shit, I thought. *Is he paying his check already?*

Instead, he handed me a folded slip of paper.

I opened it. It had a man's name and address. "Who's this?"

"That's the guy my ex cheated with," he said. "I thought about hurting him, too. I never did, but I thought about it a lot. I keep that slip as a reminder I'm stronger than the impulse."

I could've stood and hugged Paul in that Irish pub. He got it. He understood the rage — the twisted belief that hurting the other

29

guy might ease the pain.

When you say something you thought was shameful and someone replies, "Dude, same," it feels like they just unlocked a door you didn't realize you were trapped behind.

That's connection.

That's the good stuff.

Keep those people around.

Connection doesn't need originality. It needs honesty.

When you drop the mask and tell the truth, two things happen:

1. You stop judging yourself so harshly.
2. People stop seeing a performer and start seeing a person.

The most magnetic people aren't the most charismatic; they're the most real.

They say things like:

- "I fucked that up."
- "I used to think that way, too."
- "I struggle with that shit all the time."

That's power.

And it's not just friendship that thrives through honesty — leadership does, too.

In my 30s, I worked as a director of security, leading a team of about thirty officers, supervisors, and managers.

During a staff meeting, I addressed a weak spot in our incident reporting and told the team, "We have to do better, and that starts with me. I'll step up as a manager, and I need each of you to do your part, too."

I didn't think much of it then; I was just stating facts.

Later, a senior supervisor stopped by my office and said, "I've never heard a manager admit they needed to improve. Not once. You're the kind of leader I want to become."

You're Not a Freak; You're a Man in Progress

There's no shame in that.

The only shame is pretending you've arrived when it's obvious you haven't.

I used to hide everything:

- The anxiety I felt before social situations.
- The way I spiraled after rejection.
- The deep fear I'd never be good enough.

Once I stopped hiding and started telling the truth, I realized that everyone's carrying something. Some of us just hide it better than others.

Honesty is what set me free.

Your Struggles Are an Invitation to Connect

Finding your voice in private gives you the confidence to speak up in public. Vulnerability isn't weakness; it's a bridge to real connection.

Why are there so many tears in support groups?

Because for many people, it's the first time they've spoken their truth in front of someone who truly understands.

It's their first chance to connect — to be real about what they've carried in silence.

Some of the hardest cries in those rooms come from men.

Once one guy lets a tear slip, it gives the others permission to do the same. After years of being told to be stoic, they finally get to show their true selves, not the men they were told to be.

When you open up, you encourage other men to do the same.

You become the guy people feel safe being real around.

They don't trust you because you're perfect; they trust you because you're honest.

There's no Big Dick Energy in pretending to be perfect.

There's massive Big Dick Energy in owning your imperfection.

Want to make a real impact?

Be the guy who says, "I know how you feel. I've been there too."

Your Turn: Drop the Armor

Here's a challenge to prove how not-alone you really are. Don't overthink it. Just do it.

1. **Text a friend and share one thing you're struggling with right now: no sugarcoating, just honesty.**

2. **Write down three things you once thought were yours alone, but now realize are shared experiences.**

3. **Start a real conversation with someone (ideally not a stranger at the bar) and admit something that makes you uncomfortable.**

   Nothing dramatic. Just a shot of truth.
   Something like:
   "Most days, I'm just winging it."
   "Lately, I've been feeling lost."
   "I'm carrying some guilt I don't talk about."

Now watch what happens. (Spoiler: they won't run. They'll probably lean in. Maybe even tell you their truth, too.)

The part of you you're afraid to show? It might be the exact thing that warms someone else up in that freezing room. That's real power. And it doesn't have to be perfect — it just has to be honest.

Chapter Five
The Mask of Ego

My chaotic childhood ensured I'd carry deep insecurities into adulthood. I was a welfare kid raised in violent drug houses and foster homes, a weirdo who got bullied at each of my several new schools each year until seventh grade, and a dreamer who wet the bed into his teens. I didn't graduate high school with the tools to succeed. But I did have an athletic 190-pound frame, a fire to outrun my perceived destiny of a life of failure, and a stubborn refusal to believe my childhood would define my adulthood.

As a kid, I dreamed of becoming a professional wrestler. Thanks to WWE Hall of Famer Harley Race and my trainer, Derek Stone, that dream came true when I was twenty.

I was the first graduate of the Harley Race Wrestling Academy and became a high-flying babyface (the good guy fans rally behind) as I battled bigger, more experienced opponents. For the first time, I felt accepted, not just by the crowd but by the tight-knit brotherhood of wrestlers.

I found moderate success: a solid rep on the indie scene, a couple of WWE TV matches that got praise from my heroes, and a few underwhelming Japan tours. My name was in the same magazines I'd devoured as a kid.

My wrestling persona, Matt "The Missile" Murphy, and later the cocky heel "All That" Matt Murphy, became my identity. Underneath the tanned skin and purple crushed-velvet tights, I built a robust ego to shield the real me, a deeply insecure reject, from being exposed.

Here's a fun little story that shows just how far up my own ass I was during my wrestling days.

On the small-time independent scene, the ring crew was usually just the performers (wrestlers, refs, and announcers) and a few hangabouts. It was grunt work, and I'd decided I was too talented to be bothered with it.

Before a show in 2002, I was doing my usual routine of walking with fake urgency to look like I was on my way to do something important when I passed a flatbed trailer stacked with pieces of the ring. A man picked up one end of a support beam and locked eyes with me, expecting me to grab the other. The second our eyes met, I was grateful it was reality that hit me with a right cross and not him.

The man was Leon Spinks, a former world boxing champion. He was booked for a guest appearance that night, but when he saw there was work to be done, he jumped in without hesitation. This guy beat Muhammad Ali, and he sure as hell didn't act like he was too good to help set up the ring. Who the fuck was I to think I was?

It humbled me enough that from then on, I helped set up and tear down the ring at every indie show I worked.

But there was an even heavier dose of humbling just around the corner.

A car accident caused a neck injury that ended my four-year wrestling career, which had likely plateaued anyway unless I'd shown more dedication in the gym. When it was gone, so was my identity.

In the months after the wreck, I searched for meaning — and wrote a book about my climb from a group foster home to the squared circle. A company posing as a traditional publisher (which

I'd later realize was just a slick vanity press) released it in 2005. Six months later, I waited eagerly for my first royalty check, hungry for validation and ready to laugh in the faces of everyone who'd doubted me. When the envelope arrived, I tore it open like it was going to change my life. It did — just not in the way I expected. Thirteen. Fucking. Dollars.

What the fuck? I thought. Humiliation burned through me. That's impossible. *Is that all my life story is worth? Is that all* I'm *worth?*

Stripped of my career and robbed of validation, I was left with a bloated ego and a gnawing fear that I'd already peaked — in my early twenties.

When You Get Your Confidence from Wish, You Get Ego

Ego and confidence aren't the same thing. Hell, they're practically opposites.

An egotistical man pretends and fears being found out; a confident man is real and has nothing to hide.

An egotistical man tries to control the narrative; a confident man lets the truth speak for itself.

An egotistical man has Small Dick Energy. A confident man? Big Dick Energy, no question.

For too long, I confused my ego for confidence.

There was a time I thought I was the man. As a pro wrestler, I got plenty of free drinks and attention from women. People saw me as successful — hell, I saw me as successful.

I thought I had confidence, but underneath, I felt like shit about myself. Like pro wrestling, ego is all smoke and mirrors. It sells the illusion.

Confidence is built brick by brick. Ego is a knock-off you settle for when you skip the grind and tell yourself it's "close enough."

When your self-image is a pile of shit, ego is the cologne you use to mask the odor, and confidence is the soap you use to actually clean it up.

Real confidence isn't propped up by praise. It's not tied to your relationship or your Likes on social media. If it vanishes the second one of those gets taken away, it wasn't confidence at all. It was ego in a mask.

And when the masks — or purple crushed-velvet tights — come off, the guys faking it panic.

Your Ego Is Full of Shit

Ego: "You've gotta prove you're the smartest, strongest, and best."

Confidence: "If you're the smartest person in the room, you need to find another room or you'll never grow."

Ego: "If they don't like you, you don't matter."

Confidence: "Their opinions of me are none of my business."

Ego: "Never show weakness."

Confidence: "It's okay not to know. That's how you learn."

Ego: "You're only as good as your last win."

Confidence: "You gave it hell, even if you fell short."

Ego: "You have to prove your value."

Confidence: "Your worth isn't up for debate."

One of the most liberating things I've ever done was admit how full of shit I was.

That my persona was a mask.

That my bravado was nothing but armor.

That my self-worth was something I measured by my accomplishments.

Once I let that façade crumble, I found someone underneath worth knowing. Flawed, anxious, and unsure — but honest, resilient, and way more likable than the character I used to play.

The crowd may be gone. The tights are packed away. But what's left is something stronger than applause: me, unmasked, and finally at peace with who I am.

When Ego Drives, You Crash

I've lost great women because my ego couldn't handle being wrong. I've missed out on real opportunities because I thought certain tasks were beneath me. I've torched bridges just to avoid hearing hard truths.

Every man has. But we rarely talk about it because we're taught to be tough, not truthful.

But real strength? It's owning your shit: no excuses, no spin, just facing it like a man.

A confident man says, "Yeah, I screwed up. What can I learn from it?"

An egotistical man says, "I didn't do anything wrong. Why am I getting blamed?"

Guess which one people respect, follow, and want in their corner.

Your Confidence Is Built, Not Born

If you feel like you don't have it yet, that's good. That means you're not faking it. Confidence is a process — a muscle you build by showing up, messing up, and learning.

You build it by:
- Doing things that scare you just enough.
- Telling the truth, even when it's uncomfortable.
- Admitting when you don't know something.
- Sincerely apologizing when you've wronged someone.
- Letting people see the real you.

Every time you show your true self, you chip away at ego and make space for real confidence to grow.

Now it's your turn. Drop the act. Face the mirror.

Your Turn: Ego Inventory

Before we dive in, here's the one rule that matters: be honest with yourself. No ego, no self-deception; it's just you and the truth, face to face. That's how real change starts.

Take five to ten minutes and answer these questions. I'll get the party started and add mine.

1. Where in your life are you putting on a show?

I'm performing at work. Business has been slow, and I'm trying to keep my stress out of my sales pitches.

2. What's something you tend to hide or exaggerate?

I hide my wrestling past by skipping it entirely. Most people I've met in the last five years don't even know I worked in the wrestling business. It played a role in shaping the man I've become, but it's not who I am now, and I'd rather not confuse the two.

3. When was the last time you owned a mistake without making excuses?

I'm in a healthy relationship, so I often admit when I'm wrong without excuses. The one time I struggled was when I startled my girlfriend, waking her from a nap. She snapped at me; I reacted defensively. I took a few minutes alone, came back, and we both apologized.

4. Who are you trying to impress instead of connecting with?

I try too hard to impress my girlfriend's sister and brother-in-law. She went through hell with her ex, so I get why they might have been skeptical. I've spent more energy trying to prove I'm safe and good to her than just letting them get to know the real me.

Don't judge your answers. Just be honest. You're not exposing weakness but mapping your path to real growth and healthy confidence.

A confident man doesn't need to be the loudest voice in the

room. He doesn't have to win every argument or prove his worth to anyone. He's steady, grounded, and real. He knows who he is, and he owns it. Letting go of your ego is how that kind of energy takes root.

Confidence doesn't follow a script; it just tells the truth.

Truth is the foundation of Big Dick Energy. Without it, you're just another guy in a mask.

Chapter Six
Honesty:
The Taint Below Big Dick Energy

Most people will never see your taint. That's probably for the best. But it's a critical part of your anatomy. The perineum supports your pelvic floor, controls bodily functions, and helps with erections and orgasms. It's the unsung hero of your underwear zone. If your balls are confidence and your asshole is ego, then truth is the taint that separates them. Not glamorous, but essential to Big Dick Energy.

I know a guy who's a big fucking liar. I'd rather not, but sometimes life hands you a front-row ticket to the bullshit. If he's talking, he's lying; it's like he thinks it's a sport. He might think he's winning, but the scoreboard exists only in his mind, and it's laughably easy for anyone to check the box score. He's a husband, father, and business owner, but sometimes, he reminds me of that toddler on "America's Funniest Home Videos" who denies he stole a treat from the cookie jar while his face is covered in chocolate. It'd be hilarious if his lies didn't screw up people's lives, but lying is his default setting.

Let's get this straight: if you can't be honest, you don't have Big Dick Energy.

Lying — to others or yourself — is the native tongue of insecurity. And insecurity is the opposite of confidence.

Big Dick Energy doesn't hide behind excuses, ego, or a polished act. It steps into the light, balls out, flaws and all, and says, "This is who I am."

Most men lie because they fear rejection, judgment, admitting mistakes, or looking weak. So they perform, manipulate, and contort themselves into what they think others (especially women) want. In the process, they lose their power.

You don't have to be perfect. Just be real.
Don't want a relationship? Say so.
Feeling insecure? Own it.
Screwed up? Admit it.
Still healing? Be upfront.

Not looking for love? Don't fake it just to get laid or avoid being alone. Healthy women cherish honest men and have no interest in bullshit. Think she won't respect, "I'm not looking for anything serious"? Try her. She might walk, but that's better than playing a game you'll both lose.

Want to be a man of value? Be a man of truth.

The guys who get the most respect — the ones with peace, real love, and magnetic presence — aren't bullshitters.
They're consistent.
Their word is solid.
Their values show up in how they speak and act.
They don't shape-shift.
They don't ghost to avoid hard conversations.
They don't manipulate to get their needs met.
They shoot straight.
They own their shit.

Big Dick Energy doesn't lie; it doesn't have to.

If you're building a better version of yourself, start with the truth. That's the foundation of confidence.

That's where real growth begins.

"Why" Your Way to the Truth

"Are you trolling?" I asked Ben, my therapist, during my first divorce. "It feels like you're mocking me."

"Why?" Ben asked. There it was again — that fucking question. It was about the only word he'd used during the session. At $140 an hour, my patience was wearing thin.

But there was a method to his madness. Although I didn't see it at the time, he was peeling back the layers of my bullshit to get to the truth — one why at a time.

Here's how it works.

Let's say you're having a drink at a bar after a long week. Some loudmouth across the bar calls you a pussy loud enough for everyone to hear. Your instinct is to stand up and prove him wrong.

This is where the question comes in — the question that has the power to excavate truth from beneath ego:

Why?

Why do I want to fight him? Because he disrespected me.

Why does disrespect bother me? Because it makes me feel powerless.

Why do I fear feeling powerless? Because if I'm powerless, I'm helpless — and hopeless.

Why do I associate violence with strength? Because growing up, I watched helplessly as my mom's husband physically abused her. I was too small and too weak to do anything about it. Now that I'm bigger and stronger, I can protect myself and those I love.

Now we're getting somewhere.

The urge to fight really isn't about the stranger at the bar. It's about a boy who couldn't defend his mom from an evil man. It's about inherited definitions of masculinity — ones that equate power with dominance, dignity with aggression. It's about a man trying to outrun a shame he never asked for but still carries.

Most men live at the surface of their emotions, reacting rather than reflecting. But when you peel back each layer with another why, you start to see that the truth beneath the surface is rarely the same as the initial feeling.

What starts as rage might be fear.

What feels like strength might just be a shield guarding your trauma.

Peeling back those layers is uncomfortable. It strips away the excuses we use to justify our actions and reactions, and it confronts us with the possibility that what we've called manhood might be a disguise for our insecurity.

But it's also freeing.

When you get to the core of why you feel what you feel, you reclaim power over your choices. This leads to better choices and confident accountability. You no longer have to brawl your way through discomfort.

You can choose not to fight the man at the bar — not because you're scared, but because you refuse to follow a script for masculinity you didn't write. His insult traveled to you at the speed of sound; let it fall off you just as quickly.

It starts with a single word:

Why?

The Myth of "My Truth"

Let's bust this myth: there's no "your truth" or "my truth." There's just the truth. Everything else is perspective, fogged up by emotion.

Don't get it twisted: your experience matters, and your feelings are valid. But your emotional interpretation isn't the same as factual reality. The moment you dress up your opinion as objective truth, you're not being deep. You're being delusional.

Here's what "my truth" often sounds like:
- I was the only one trying in the relationship.
- I was disrespected because she disagreed with me in front of her dad.
- I was pissed, so nothing I said should count.

"My truth" culture might reward you online with sympathy, clout, or viral attention. But once your post fades into obscurity, you're left with reality. It's not empowerment; it's a hall pass to dismiss facts that don't feed your narrative — a lie your ego is selling you.

Here's the problem: truth doesn't care how you feel. You might *feel* betrayed; that doesn't mean someone betrayed you. You might *think* the world's against you; that doesn't make you oppressed. Feelings matter, but they aren't facts.

Important side note, fellas: This section is for informational purposes and should only be applied to your own life. It should not be weaponized to dismiss others' feelings. For the love of God, never say 'truth doesn't care how you feel' to someone who's mid-tears — I've got the divorce papers to prove it.

If everyone gets to define their own truth, then truth means nothing. If everything's true, nothing is.

Truth — real truth — isn't personal. It's observable. It's consistent. It stands up even when your emotions don't. It's gravity, not vibe.

Growth starts when you stop obsessing over your story and face reality.

You don't get to say, "I'm doing my best," if your actions are torching every bridge.

You don't get to hide behind "my truth" if you haven't sorted through your wounds, projections, and bullshit.

There's nothing brave about clinging to "your truth." Real courage is staring down the sometimes ugly, inconvenient, unforgiving truth.

Speak your perspective. Share your story. Own your shit.

But don't confuse feelings with facts. Don't sell opinion as gospel.

Truth doesn't bend to your story. You either face it or stay broken.

Audit the Truth You Remember

On Christmas Day, 1985, my brother Shane and I — eight and six years old — rode a city bus with our mom to the Salvation Army in Phoenix. We had a hot meal, and afterward, each kid got to pick one toy.

I picked a green wind-up truck you'd rev by pushing forward, then release to watch it trudge across the carpet. I loved that thing.

For nearly forty years, I remembered the green truck as the only gift I received that Christmas. I told the story often, usually when preaching about gratitude.

At forty-four, while I told my girlfriend, Shara (more on her later), the story before our first Christmas together, something clicked: the story wasn't true. I hadn't lied — I'd just remembered it wrong. The real memory came back.

Here's what really happened.

A week or two before Christmas, Shane and I were home alone. Mom's abusive second husband had just been thrown in jail (again), and she was out for the day.

Shane hatched a plan: "Let's open our Christmas presents." He was my big brother; I'd've gone along with anything he suggested. We ripped open every gift.

When Mom got home, she was furious to find Shane and me sitting in the living room, playing with our new toys, but she didn't take them away. And to make sure we each got something on Christmas Day, she took us to the Salvation Army. By then, I'd forgotten why we didn't have presents under our tree.

It took almost four decades for the truth to emerge.

The truth never changed, only my memory.

Sometimes, finding truth means looking at old memories with fresh eyes. You'll be surprised by what you might find.

Ready to Face the Truth?

In your journey to find truth, it's important to set aside prejudices about how you remember things. Sometimes, we bury the truth; other times, people bury it for us.

Self-deception isn't just a bad habit; it's a full-fledged prison cell. Want freedom? Break the lock by asking yourself:

1. What truth would finally set me free if I had the balls to admit it?

2. Which memories am I clinging to that no longer pass muster?

3. Who gets a version of me that's edited for approval?

Own truth like your confidence depends on it.

Without the taint of truth in the middle, you're just a dick and an asshole with nothing holding you together.

Chapter Seven
Find the Voice That Sounds Like You

Confidence isn't something you can fake; you don't get it by striking a pose in the mirror or curating the perfect post. It's built one raw, uncomfortable moment at a time.

You earn it when you:

- Ask for help when you'd rather tough it out.
- Apologize without excuses.
- Choose integrity over acceptance.
- Walk away from toxicity, whether it's a job, a relationship, a friend, or a relative, even when fear begs you to stay.

These days, too many people treat confidence like a participation trophy, something you deserve just for existing instead of growing. That kind of hollow confidence is a fragile shell of filters, Likes, follows, and micro-dosed dopamine hits. It crumbles under pressure.

Real confidence is a muscle. It grows when you do the harder thing, the thing your ego resists. It's not instant gratification, but it will last. Build it on truth, integrity, and humility, and it will stand. Build it on presentation, possessions, and online praise, and it will collapse.

Social media magnifies the problem. Some influencers have genuine confidence and use their platforms to create meaningful or profitable work that connects with people. But others measure their worth by follower counts and reaction metrics. When that artificial validation slows or stops, their "confidence" goes with it.

Confidence begins the second you drop the act.

You'll stumble. You'll say something real and get blank stares. Something like, "I didn't just lose her to another man. I lost her to the man she begged me to be." It'll feel uncomfortable. That's how you know you're getting closer.

You start sounding more like you, and less like everyone else.

At its core, confidence is this: knowing and owning your voice.

The Voice You Were Taught vs. The Voice That's Yours

At some point, every man needs to ask himself:

Whose voice is this in my head, and when did I start mistaking it for mine?

Maybe it's your dad telling you to wipe your tears and "be a man."

Maybe it's a coach saying you're not good enough to make the team.

Maybe it's an ex whispering that you were never enough.

Or maybe it's your own voice, trained over decades to perform to fit the world's expectations.

Whatever it is, if you're going to build real, unshakable confidence — the kind that stands tall after getting knocked down — you have to find your voice.

Not the loudest.

Not the most agreeable.

The truest.

Growing up, I learned a voice that said:

"To be accepted, you have to stand out."

"To be valuable, you have to be special."

"To stay safe, you have to act strong and bury your weaknesses."

So, I tried to become the guy people liked: the funny one, the hard worker, the peacekeeper — and for a while, the guy in crushed-velvet wrestling tights.

That voice got me acceptance, but not peace.

It got me attention, but often the wrong kind.

It got me laid, but not loved.

You can't fully receive love if you don't love yourself.

And you can't love yourself if you're hiding him.

Your Voice Doesn't Need an Audience

Once I started figuring out who I really was, my behavior changed. I wasn't trying so hard to impress anyone.

I wore what I liked, not what kept me safe from disapproval or mockery. These days, I'll walk into a biker bar in a Hawaiian shirt and khaki shorts. If someone has a problem with it, that's their problem. (Bikers don't care — most have a couple of Hawaiian shirts in their closets, too).

I started speaking directly instead of dancing around people's feelings. I'm not an unfiltered asshole — those guys are exhausting — but I'll tell the truth, even if it ruffles feathers.

I didn't need agreement from everyone or to be the funniest or most liked. I wasn't trying to be a comic or a politician. I wasn't trying to win the room anymore; I was just trying to be in it as myself.

That's when people started responding on a deeper level, because nothing is more magnetic than someone who's fully themselves.

In the age of curated feeds and filtered personalities, we're starving for something real. Be the guy who delivers it.

Let's be honest: most men are performing. We cycle through roles — provider, protector, clown, intellectual, stoic — depending on who's watching. It's a survival skill in a world that rewards conformity.

But eventually, you have to ask yourself:

Do I want to be liked for a façade or loved for who I truly am?

What Your Voice Sounds Like

Here's what it sounds like when a man speaks in his true voice:

- He says, "I don't know," and doesn't flinch.
- He says, "That's not for me," without explaining himself.
- He says, "I'm angry" or "I'm hurting" without apology.
- He's direct, not a dick.
- He stands tall even when someone disagrees.

You might not be there yet, and that's okay.

Finding your voice is about unlearning the bullshit to become who you really are.

The Practice: Tune Into You

If you want to find your voice, start here:

1. Silence the noise.

Spend ten minutes daily with no music, scrolling, or distractions. Get quiet.

2. Say what you think out loud.

Even if it's clunky. *Especially* if it's clunky. Practice in low-stakes moments until it feels natural.

3. Write like nobody's reading.

Journal with zero filter. Say the dark, messy, weird, hilarious stuff you'd never post.

4. Own your preferences.

Don't pretend to like something to fit in. Say you hate Marvel movies if you do. Say you love Nickelback if you do. No shame.

5. Disagree respectfully.

Speak up when it matters. Learn to be disagreeable without being an asshole.

Your Voice, Your Power

When you find your voice, you tap into real power.

People respect it, not because it's the loudest or the smartest, but because it's honest.

And honesty is rare.

You don't need to shout to be heard.

You don't need to dominate to feel strong.

You don't need to be perfect to be accepted.

You just need to be unapologetically you — not obnoxiously or aggressively, but honestly.

Big Dick Energy isn't about being bold just to be loud.

It's about being real in a world hooked on fakery.

And there's nothing more powerful than a man who finally learns to speak in his own voice.

Be a Voice of Reason, But Never a Voice of Doubt

One of my many mistakes in my first marriage was silencing my wife's singing voice.

We were driving home from the grocery store. Metallica was on the radio, and she sang along.

"Who sings this?" I asked.

"Metallica," she said, shooting me a look; she knew I listened to them often.

"Cool," I said. "We should let Metallica sing it." It was meant to be funny. But it embarrassed her.

And from that day on, for the rest of our marriage, she never sang in front of me again.

Singing brings people joy. And I took that from her with one dumb wisecrack. I never got that part of her back.

Don't fucking be the reason someone stops singing, dancing, or showing who they are.

Never be the voice of doubt in someone's head. Be a voice of reason: that trusted friend, partner, or parent who challenges you with love.

A voice of doubt says:

- "Why would anyone want to read your book?"
- "Sounds like you've found your next ex."
- "Your last business failed. This one will too."

A voice of reason says:

- "I know you're pumped about your new book, but maybe give it one more round of edits before calling it done."
- "It's awesome you're excited about her, but take your time. Make sure she's consistent through the honeymoon phase before you dive in too deep."
- "You've got a strong idea and passion, but start it as a side hustle so you're building something, not betting everything."

Don't be the reason someone goes quiet. And never someone else be the reason *you* do.

Chapter Eight
Respect — The Real Alpha Trait

Don't think, just answer: Would you rather be feared or respected?

If you choose "feared," you're on the wrong track.

Fear gets you silence, distance, and people pretending to like you until you leave the room.

We've reached a fascinating time in the evolution of masculinity. The tug-of-war between alpha dick-waggers and beta dick-tuckers has left the rest of us wondering what the hell being a man is supposed to look like.

The whole "alpha male" thing? The façade has been exposed; people can see through it. Real alphas don't bark, flex, or try to win every room. They're not out to dominate; they're in control of themselves and don't need to control others. That's what makes them powerful.

Equally exhausting are the beta males who cower away from their own nature. Not gay or trans men — I mean phonies who sneer at masculinity, not because they've outgrown it, but because they've never had any of their own.

You want Big Dick Energy? Start with respect.

Give it. Earn it. Keep it.

Respect is the quiet superpower. It makes people lean in, trust you, follow you, and feel safe. It's what separates real men from posers. It's what makes your presence powerful, even in silence.

The Problem with the "Alpha" Myth

The modern "alpha male" has become a parody of masculinity: all noise, no substance. It's grown men cosplaying toughness while steamrolling over others, cranking the machismo dial up to fifteen, and throwing their backs out to drag their knuckles. It's embarrassing to witness.

Here are some examples:

- Crushing beer cans like it's an Olympic sport (if a toddler can do it, it's not that impressive).
- Bragging about bar fights.
- Revving engines or squealing tires.
- Mocking any man who doesn't perform masculinity their way.
- Refusing to help around the house because it's "women's work."

If it screams "I'm a man" while doing the bare minimum, it's performance, not confidence.

The so-called alpha dominates; it needs you to shrink to feel tall. The real man stands up and helps others rise with him. True confidence doesn't require putting anyone down. When you know your power, you don't fear someone else's.

Last year, I was drinking with my girlfriend Shara at a dive bar when Tenacious D's "Fuck Her Gently" came on the jukebox.

"Your guy looks like he fucks gently," some dude said to her from across the bar. His buddy laughed.

I sipped my beer. It wasn't fear that kept me quiet, just zero interest in acknowledging him. His opinion of my sex game was as irrelevant as he was.

Moments like that prove you don't need to puff your chest or throw punches to win. Real strength is knowing when someone isn't worth y—

"Where are your women?" Shara shot back.

Silence.

Game. Set. Match.

The rules didn't say she had to stand for it.

So, you're a tough guy, huh? Fun fact: as an adult man, you're more likely to get food poisoning than to get into a fist fight this year. There's value in being able to protect yourself and others, but there's greater value in being calm and resourceful during a crisis — and avoiding undercooked food.

If Masculinity Can Evolve in Pro Wrestling, It Can Evolve Anywhere

Once a caricature of performative toughness, pro wrestling has quietly pulled off one of the most unexpected evolutions in modern masculinity. The old-school image of jacked-up guys shouting about violence and dominance has given way to something far more human.

Today, top stars talk openly about their real-life struggles, showing their humanity while still getting you excited for their upcoming WrestleMania matches. Many of today's top performers aren't just admired for their physiques and in-ring skills but respected for their honesty, empathy, and a connection that hits deeper than the old "I'm the toughest guy here" routine.

Respect is Commanded, Not Demanded

Isn't it adorable that people who've done the least to earn respect are the most sensitive to perceived disrespect? It's never the man whose life is firing on all cylinders who blows up over nothing.

Let me say it plainly: If you need to demand respect, you probably don't deserve it. *Demanding* respect means you try using force to gain it. *Commanding* respect means the quality of your actions and words earns it from people.

You earn respect by:

- Keeping your word and showing up when you say you will.
- Listening more than you talk.
- Treating people with dignity, from CEOs to busboys.
- Being the same man in private as you are in public.

It takes emotional maturity to lead with respect, especially when it's not convenient or expected.

Real confidence doesn't punch down. It doesn't mock, belittle, or dismiss.

The more secure you are, the more grace you give.

A man with Big Dick Energy gives respect without needing a reason. He doesn't take cheap shots at people who can't fight back — because of their job, age, or the fact that they're just a screen name.

Anything less is a weak-ass beta move.

Respect in Relationships: Stop Performing, Start Showing Up

Let's talk about romantic respect; too many men fall flat here.

Respect isn't showing up with flowers on Valentine's Day but tuning out the other 364.

It's not masking your anger with silence or your insecurity with control.

Real respect means:

- You listen when she speaks, even when it's uncomfortable.

If it matters enough for her to share it, it damn sure better matter enough for you to listen.

- You don't interrupt or roll your eyes when she opens up.

Looking for the fastest way to get dumped? Dismiss her feelings like they're an inconvenience.

- You own your shit — no gaslighting, no spin.

It takes real balls to look her in the eye and say, "I fucked up.

I'm sorry. What can I do to make it right?"
- You treat her like an equal, not a project, a child, or a prize.

If you treat your partner like she's less capable or less worthy, start budgeting for single life. That mindset leads straight to loneliness and bulk lotion.

Big Dick Energy isn't performative, but if it were, trusting your partner would be a huge flex. Showing the confidence in yourself, your lady, and your relationship to make her feel free to express herself in the way she dresses or have a night out with her friends is critical to having a relationship rooted in respect.

This might blow up in your face — or just speed up an inevitable break-up. Some will take advantage of trust and kindness; that's their brokenness to fix. Stay the course. The right one will appreciate it.

If that sounds soft to you, congrats: you've been sold a lie about what strength really is.

You know who's stronger than me? Most women.

Yeah, they may cry more. That's not weakness; that's processing.

Think about everything women carry, give, and endure. They've already lapped us, and that's before you even factor in childbirth.

You want to spot a strong man? Look at how his woman carries herself.

Watch their energy. She's glowing. He's present.

He opens doors, pulls out chairs, and holds eye contact when she talks.

Meanwhile, the "alphas" mutter, "He should take his balls out of her purse."

And while they sulk and sip, that man is building love — and they're just building resentment.

It takes way more strength to build a woman up than to tear her down.

Weak men fear strong women. Not the assholes screaming at

fast-food clerks — the ones who walk into a room calm, grounded, and clear on who the fuck they are.

They've got boundaries, standards, and zero interest in babysitting your fragile ego.

There's nothing sexier than a woman with Big Dick Energy. Period.

The Difference Between Healthy Masculinity and Toxic Masculinity

Let's clear something up: masculinity isn't the problem.
Masculinity has built civilizations and protected families.
We don't owe the world an apology for being men.
But masculinity without introspection? That's where shit goes sideways.

Toxic masculinity isn't building muscles, drinking bourbon, or watching football.
It's not stoicism under pressure or assertiveness in a world that eats the timid.
None of that's toxic; it's just male.

Toxic masculinity is insecurity dressed up as dominance.
It's the guy who calls empathy weakness.
The one who measures worth by body count or bank balance.
Controls others instead of mastering himself.
Tells his partner how to dress.
Refuses to apologize, admit fault, or shut up long enough to actually listen.
Toxic masculinity? Pure Small Dick Energy.

When toxic masculinity turns violent — especially toward a spouse or child — that's No Dick Energy.
"I lost control" is a coward's excuse.
Let's be real: if Dwayne Johnson had been in the room, even the most hot-headed man would have found a way to keep his composure.

It's telling how selective "losing control" can be.

Healthy masculinity is a whole different beast.
It's strong and soft. Bold and kind. Disciplined and vulnerable.
It's the protector who doesn't need to control.
The dad who listens as much as he leads.
The man who cries when he needs to and doesn't apologize for it.
It's not a show. It's not insecure.
It doesn't shrink others to feel tall.
Toxic masculinity is ego-driven.
Healthy masculinity is confidence-driven.

The low point of my masculinity was in the mid-2010s. Mind you, this is when I was a security director and led courses on defensive tactics, use of force, and making arrests — "manly" shit. I went at least three years without crying, including after my mom's death and during her funeral. I mistook stoicism for strength, vulnerability for weakness. Unsurprisingly, this is also when my first wife gave up on our marriage.

Too many men have grown up thinking we're only allowed a few emotions: anger, pride, lust, and hunger. Everything else — sadness, fear, anxiety, grief — gets dismissed as feelings "for pussies." That's the kind of thinking that leads to broken homes, buried trauma, and men dying younger than they should because they refuse to ask for help.
We're not weaker for being human but stronger for owning our humanity.

Evolving as a man doesn't mean neutering yourself.
It doesn't mean apologizing for being male or pretending testosterone is toxic by default.
You can still be the hunter, the builder, and the protector.
Just do it without dragging your knuckles.
You can be fierce when it's called for and still be gentle when needed.

You can handle conflict as it arises and still lead with collaboration.

You can cry at a Subaru commercial and still bench press like a boss.

You can be competitive, assertive, and sensitive.

Being a man isn't the problem.

Being emotionally tone-deaf and ego-driven is.

You don't have to shrink.

You just have to evolve.

Just because you listen to, openly share with, encourage, uplift, and respect others (or cry while watching The Notebook) doesn't mean you're soft.

You can be sensitive and still embrace your strength. You can be supportive and still have a competitive streak. You can still be a man.

You simply need to be accountable and aware of how your actions impact others. You must build, not destroy.

But damn it, you have to evolve.

> *A man who views the world the same at 50*
> *as he did at 20 has wasted 30 years of his life.*
> –Muhammad Ali

We don't need more men trying to dominate.

We need more men willing to inspire.

Less obsession with being "alpha."

More devotion to being authentic.

The world doesn't need less masculinity.

It needs better masculinity.

And if that pisses someone off, good.

That means we're getting close to the truth.

Some people of both genders seek to disempower men, to shame us for being men. Those are weaklings who overcompensate by shouting us down.

Strong women are a fucking treasure. Weak women feel inferior and campaign to disempower men instead of growing strong enough to stand tall beside them.

Weak men apologize for being born males because rejection of their identity is easier than digging to their cores and making meaningful changes.

You can't fix those people — no one can — so treat them like the white noise they are.

We're not sorry for being men.
But we are responsible for becoming better ones.

The Inner Game: Self-Respect First

Here's the part most guys miss:
You can't give real respect to others if you don't give it to yourself first. The same can be said for love.

Self-respect means:

- Setting and holding boundaries.
- Walking away from disrespect.
- Refusing scraps in love, work, or your relationship with yourself.
- Standing by your values, even if you're the only one.

Note: The last one hits hard right now. At work, I built my reputation on integrity and credibility, and customers rewarded me with their loyalty. The business has evolved, and customer loyalty has nearly vanished in the industry in recent years due to a complete change in how they consume our products and services. It's not the customers' fault; it's simply become a transactional business where it means little who's selling or what they stand for.

Self-respect doesn't come from how others treat you.
It comes from how you treat yourself.
Raise the bar.

Watch your confidence rise with it.

Your Turn: Build Your Respect Muscles

Here's your challenge for the week:

1. Give someone unexpected respect.

Ask a shy or new co-worker for their opinion. Watch how it lands.

2. Enforce one boundary you've been avoiding.

Whether it's saying "no" to a favor or telling someone you need space, set the bar higher for how you're treated.

3. Clean up one mess.

Apologize for something you know you screwed up. No excuses. No justifications. Just own it. That's respect in action.

Respect is the real flex.

It lets you be heard without shouting, love without controlling, and live without chasing approval.

Big Dick Energy isn't about dominance.

It's about respect — for yourself, and for everyone you meet.

And when you lead with that, people don't just follow you; they feel you.

Fear fades the second you leave the room.

Respect stays.

Big Dick Energy is mastering the presence that makes people stand taller when you walk in — and glad they met you when you walk out.

Chapter Nine
Forgive Like a Man with BDE

Forgiveness isn't weakness. It's one of the boldest, hardest, most grounded choices a man can make. It's not about letting people off the hook or forgetting, and it's definitely not about being a doormat. Forgiveness is about reclaiming your peace without handing over your power.

Forgiving Others Without Losing Yourself

Let's be real: people will hurt you. Sometimes by accident, sometimes on purpose. When that happens, you've got a choice. You can carry that pain into every relationship, every room, every damn conversation — or you can face it, feel it, and let it go.

Forgiveness doesn't say what they did was okay. It says, I'm not letting this own me anymore.

Holding onto that pain punishes you, not them. It freezes you in the moment you were wronged and steals your peace thereafter. That's not power — that's a prison.

If someone is repeatedly toxic or dangerous, forgiveness isn't an invitation back in. You can forgive and still cut them out. It's not about burying grudges; it's about building boundaries.

Forgiving Yourself Can Be the Harder Fight

Self-forgiveness is the hardest form for some men. You've fucked up. You've hurt people. You've said things you wish you could take back. You've wrecked relationships, missed your moment, spiraled when you thought you were healed, or gone back when swore you were leaving.

So have I.

One of my most shameful moments happened during my second marriage.

My son told me he was struggling with the way my wife talked to him.

I tried to talk to her about it calmly.

She exploded with anger, called him into the bedroom, and berated him for questioning her unimpeachable character.

I couldn't believe the deafening sound of my silence. This wasn't me. The me I knew would've fought an army to protect my son. But she'd long ago drained my last ounce of fight. I sat like a shell of a man while my son took the verbal beating.

A few months later, my son was living a thousand miles away with his mom.

That kind of shame will eat you alive if you let it.

But hear this: carrying guilt forever doesn't make you strong. It makes you stuck.

You won't become the man you're meant to be by hating the one you used to be. You get there by learning from it, owning it, and choosing better. That's accountability. That's growth. That's what the world — your partner, your kids, your future self — needs from you.

You can't rewrite the past. But you do get to choose what kind of man you are from this moment forward.

Ask for Forgiveness — But Know You're Not Entitled to It

If you've wronged someone, ask for forgiveness. Not with manipulation. Not with expectation. Just with truth.

For this one, you'll need your active voice, not your passive voice.

A real apology doesn't sound like "I'm sorry you were hurt." It sounds like: "I'm sorry I hurt you."

A real apology doesn't include, "I apologize," which comes across like reporting that you're performing the act of apologizing. Saying the words "I'm sorry" expresses remorse directly.

A real apology sure as hell doesn't include an aggressive, sarcastic, or insincere tone.

Say you're sorry. And then — this part's key — give them space. Don't demand forgiveness. Don't guilt them into rushing it. Don't make your healing their responsibility.

They owe you nothing. But you owe the truth.

BDE isn't about being perfect. It's about being honest, even when it costs you.

If they forgive you, be grateful. If they don't, keep doing the work anyway.

Forgiveness Isn't a Weapon

Some men use forgiveness like a power move. They say they've forgiven someone but keep dragging it out, throwing it in their face, and punishing them. That's not forgiveness. That's emotional manipulation.

Let it go or don't. But don't pretend you're the bigger person while still holding the dagger.

A man with Big Dick Energy — no, scratch that — a grown-ass man doesn't need to punish people to feel powerful.

Letting Go Is Masculine

You want to be the kind of man who can carry heavy things, right? Here's the truth: some of the heaviest shit you'll ever shoulder is emotional. And sometimes, the strongest thing you can do is set it down.

Forgiveness isn't soft.

It's saying: "That pain happened, but it doesn't get to run my life."

That's what it means to forgive like a man with BDE.

Not because you're above it, but because you've finally grown beyond needing to carry it.

When Forgiveness Comes Too Late

Sometimes, we wait too long.

We wait to say we're sorry. We wait to own our part. We wait to forgive someone who hurt us. We wait for the "right" moment to clean up the mess — until the moment's gone.

By the time we're ready, they've moved on. Or they've passed on. Or they've stopped caring whether we ever come around. That's the cost of delay. That's what it feels like when forgiveness shows up late to the party and the lights are already off.

When I worked in management, my mornings started with coffee, planning my day, and a round of Bejeweled in my recliner. One September morning in 2014, my brother texted:

"Mom was found dead this morning."

In a moment I'll regret forever, I flicked the notification away and finished my game before calling him, as if finishing that level could delay the truth.

Mom had been on Cloud Nine the night she died. She'd just been hired as an on-site manager at an assisted living facility — free apartment, steady salary. While moving her belongings in, she had a heart attack on the sidewalk. One second, on top of the world. The next, gone.

Big Dick Energy

I learned it all second-hand. We hadn't spoken in two years. She'd missed my son's sixth birthday in 2012 — no card, no call. When she finally called the next day to apologize, I let it go to voicemail. Her stumbling, nervous tone sounded like a lie.

Two weeks later, I told her how pissed I was. "I'm used to missed birthdays and empty Christmas promises," I said. "I'm used to Brenda being Brenda. But I won't let my son think that's normal."

I asked for space. She ignored it, flooding me with calls and Facebook tags until I blocked her number and deleted her.

Two years later, she was gone.

Back then, I was emotionally shut down. I felt nothing over her death — no grief, no tears — for six months. When the grief finally came, it lasted three weeks and made every breath a struggle. By the time the levee broke, the one person I wanted to talk to about my pain was gone.

Since then, I've wished she were here to see my son grow up, joke with me about chasing her divorce record, and meet the love of my life.

If you've ever carried around the weight of unsaid apologies that never left your lips or forgiveness that never entered your heart, you know how heavy it gets. You know what it does to your spirit. It festers. It follows you. It turns into shame, self-punishment, or a hollow ache that never quite goes away.

Forgiveness isn't just about them. It's about you. It's about the kind of man you want to be. Once the window closes, the only person you can make peace with is yourself. And sometimes, that's the harder conversation.

If there's someone you need to forgive, today is as good a day as any to make it happen. If there's someone you hurt, tell the truth and ask for their forgiveness, even if they're not ready to give it. If there's a grudge you've been holding, let it go. Don't wait until the apology you never gave or accepted becomes a ghost that follows you home every night.

Big Dick Energy isn't just about showing up with confidence. It's about having the integrity to face your unfinished business — while there's still time.

It's the same honesty you learned to carry back in Chapter Six

— only now, it's turned inward.

I didn't write this chapter because I nailed it. I wrote it because I learned the hard way.

Don't let your last words be too little, too late. Let them be honest, heartfelt, and clean. That's how a man with BDE forgives — and it's one of the boldest, hardest, most grounded choices you'll ever make.

Chapter Ten
Protect Your Bandwidth

Your mental bandwidth is finite. You can't stream 4K to every device in your life at once. If you waste it on background noise, the important channels lag when you need them most.

Big Dick Energy isn't about having unlimited capacity. It's about knowing where to send the full signal and where to cut the connection.

Your Signal is Limited — Use It Like It Matters

Imagine you've got 1,000 gigabytes of emotional data to last your entire life. Seems like plenty, right? But if you burn through 700 GB on junk — your ex's Instagram drama, your boss flexing a new Mercedes while you're dodging layoffs, whatever fresh dumpster fire the news is pushing — you won't have the bandwidth left when it counts.

When the network is jammed, you miss critical uploads: your partner's real needs, a friend in crisis, a kid looking for your attention.

A man with BDE runs a clean network. He doesn't let low-res problems stream in HD and doesn't waste his signal on spam downloads.

I'll Stick with Tea, Thank You

When I dipped into online dating, politics always came up. Somewhere in the early chats or over appetizers, I'd get the inevitable:

"So, are you a Democrat or a Republican?"

On one date, a Universal Studios theme park actress asked me the question over a beer.

"Neither," I said. Hoping to change the subject, I added, "Can I tell you why Jim Halpert was actually the villain in 'The Office'?"

She froze. "Wait — neither?" The way her jaw dropped, you'd think I just told her *Wicked* was mid.

"Correct," I said. "Some people like Coke. Some like Pepsi. I drink unsweetened tea, so I'm not picking between the red and blue cans. Both are just cola in different packaging to me."

I couldn't have killed the mood faster if I'd told her about my action figure collection.

Did it cost me dates? Absolutely.

Did it save my bandwidth? Hell yes.

I'm not running political updates in the background while I'm trying to connect with someone. You don't have to take the bait, either.

What Bandwidth Drain Looks Like

Here's how you know your network is getting slammed with useless traffic:

- You rehearse comebacks for arguments you'll never have.
- You keep refreshing for Likes or wondering why someone left you on Read.
- You say yes when every cell in your body is screaming no.
- You filter your every word through the approval of strangers.

- You're too mentally fried for the things that actually matter.

Trying to care about everything is like running Netflix, Fortnite, and a Zoom call all at once on hotel Wi-Fi. Something's gonna freeze.

The Happiest Men Protect Their Bandwidth

They don't run every channel at full power. They stream with purpose:

- Their values
- Their people
- Their word
- Their health
- Their peace of mind
- Their mission

They don't beg for validation; they know who they are offline.

They're not desperate to win every argument; they'd rather get it right than be right.

They don't give full bars to people who don't respect the signal.

The Bandwidth Equation

Too much data to the wrong channels = overload and anxiety.

Too little data to the right channels = apathy and disconnection.

Balanced, intentional streaming = Big Dick Energy.

Going numb isn't strength — it's just pulling the plug. BDE is about managing the flow, not shutting it off.

Run a Bandwidth Audit

Ask yourself: Who gets my signal, and who's just stealing Wi-Fi?

Loud-typing coworker?
Airplane mode.

Troll in your DMs?
Blocked at the router.

Friend who only calls when they're broke or moving?
Password changed.

Your partner's emotional needs?
Full signal.

Your ex's opinion of your new relationship?
Service canceled.

Five Ways to Boost Your Signal Strength

Write a Bandwidth Budget

1. Pick the top five priorities that deserve your energy and attention.

Anything not on the list gets throttled.

2. Go on a Notification Diet

Silence the constant pings. Every buzz is a data drain.

3. Practice Saying, "That's Not My Bandwidth"

Calmly. Without guilt. The first time you do it, you'll feel like a goddamn network admin.

4. Stop Apologizing for Taking Up Space

Every time you do, you're letting someone else control your connection.

5. Run the Five-Year Speed Test

Ask: Will this still matter in five years? If not, it's not worth five kilobytes.

The Result: A Clean, Strong Signal

When you stop streaming energy to low-value noise, everything changes.

You rest deeper.

You speak with clarity.

You move like your time matters.

You connect at full speed with the people and purposes that count.

Your bandwidth is precious. Your signal is sacred. Big Dick Energy is knowing who gets the password — and cutting off the unwanted network traffic.

Chapter Eleven
Escaping the Social Media
Comparison Trap

Once upon a time, a man's sense of self-worth came from his actions, his relationships, and the quiet pride he took in being a dependable presence in his world. Now? It's been whittled down by algorithms, Likes, and stories that disappear in 24 hours.

Today, being a man isn't about who you are but how you perform for others, and social media is the stage.

The truth is, scrolling through your feed is slowly killing your confidence. It doesn't matter how grounded you are; when you're constantly bombarded with highlight reels of other men's presentations of their idealized lives, it feels like you're falling behind.

- The 24-year-old entrepreneur making six figures a year.
- The shirtless fitness guru preaching from a cliff at sunrise.
- Your old classmate posing with his gorgeous wife and honor-roll kids on some tropical beach.

It's easy to feel like you're underachieving. Not because you're lazy or unaccomplished, but because your brain is getting hijacked by the illusion of perfection. And make no mistake: it's a fucking illusion.

One app keeps shoving a "super-dad" influencer into my feed. Today, I clicked his profile out of morbid curiosity: thirty-five unique posts in the last 24 hours. At this point, the only thing he's fathering is a steady stream of bullshit — I'm sure his kids won't forget to bring his sponsored energy drink if they decide to visit him in the nursing home one day.

You don't have to follow the people who make you feel like shit. The puppet-masters will make sure they find you anyway.

And that's the bitch of it: you can't escape it unless you stop scrolling. Your clicks, searches, likes, even how long you stare at Bluetooth speakers in Walmart — all of it feeds the beast.

These platforms know you better than your therapist. Ever seen a Prilosec ad while eating tacos? That's not random — it's precision warfare. Social giants study your cravings, target your insecurities, and inject the products straight into your feed.

That's the bait. Now here's the switch: the more your attention is shaped by algorithms, the more your identity starts to follow. You don't just act for others; you start believing that performance is who you are.

You start comparing, not because you want to, but because it's embedded in these platforms' programming. That's where performative masculinity sinks its hooks in. You don't just want to succeed; you want to be seen succeeding. You want your gains, grind, and growth to be validated and admired by people you've never met. The dopamine rush of approval is real, and it's a trap.

Even the most grounded men get pulled in.

Performative masculinity demands a version of yourself that never struggles or admits weakness. But that version isn't real; it's a cardboard cutout. The more you become that guy, the further you get from yourself.

You start hiding your fears. You bury your insecurities under Likes and comments.

But confidence built on applause? It's fragile as hell. It vanishes the second the spotlight moves on.

One day, you're the man. The next, you're invisible — and you don't know who you are without the applause.

To be clear, there's nothing wrong with having ambition or sharing your wins. But if your identity depends on the approval of strangers, you're building a mask, not confidence. And all masks, no matter how well-designed, eventually crack.

Authentic confidence is not loud or curated. It doesn't need to be broadcast. It comes from doing the hard things when no one's watching, being the same man in public as you are in private, and living a life that feels right in your gut even if it doesn't look good on Instagram.

It's not about dominance or clout; it's about substance and being who you are without having to perform it for your audience.

Feeling stuck? Here's your call to action:

- Unfollow the bullshit.
- Delete the apps if they're bringing you more despair than joy.
- Focus on your own life instead of obsessing over anyone else's.
- Rebuild your confidence offline.

You can't follow your way into becoming a man of substance; you must live it and earn it. And when you do, the world will eventually notice, not because you shouted but because you showed up authentically.

Put the damn phone down. Pick your life back up where you left it.

My Confession Before the Sin

I promised not to bullshit you, so let me be honest about something before I start sounding too self-righteous.

Before I started writing this book, I'd done an almost complete social media detox. I deleted the apps that left me feeling despair and limited my time on the others to no more than fifteen minutes a day; I didn't miss it.

This book is the start of a bigger movement — but to spread it, I have to use the very machine I just told you to unplug from.

Behind every achievement in human history lies a monster willing to do the dirty work.

Without the power of social media, this will be a one-man crusade that never builds its army, a voice shouting into the ether. Succeeding will require me to create content that finds its audience, which means I'll have to spend more time on social media.

So, I've made myself a deal:

- Never open an app without a purpose.
- Close it as soon as I'm done.
- Never let Likes define whether I succeeded.

If you want to be a pal, help me jam the algorithm. Leave reviews, tell your people, hand this book to someone who needs it. Spread Big Dick Energy in the wild. The less time I have to spend dancing for the feed, the more time I can spend living like a man.

Chapter Twelve
Fix Your Inner Circle

Big Dick Energy doesn't grow in isolation — or toxic soil.

Your confidence isn't built in a vacuum. It's shaped daily by the people around you. Your habits, mindset, and energy are molded by your environment. And too many men are trying to grow into stronger, healthier, more grounded versions of themselves while still anchored to the same tired, toxic, energy-sucking crew.

Let me put it bluntly:

You can't level up if your circle keeps dragging you down.

If your confidence is constantly under attack — if the people closest to you belittle your goals, mock your growth, or scoff at emotional openness — your inner circle is trash.

You can bench press your body weight, meditate every morning, and read all the right self-help books (hey, thanks), but if your circle stays toxic, your growth stalls. Period.

Fix that, and everything else starts to fall into place.

You Are Who You Hang With

That's not just a catchy line; it's hardwired into your psychology.

You become like the people you spend the most time with. Consciously or not, their energy, habits, beliefs, and attitudes toward growth rub off on you.

If you're hanging out with men who numb out every night, scoff at anything deeper than fantasy football, and belittle your goals because they challenge their comfort zones, guess what? That's the weight you're training in.

And eventually, it breaks you — or molds you into something you never meant to be.

Ask yourself:

- Are the people closest to me chasing growth or avoiding it?
- Do they hold me accountable or co-sign my bullshit?
- Do they challenge me or just keep me comfortable?
- Do they make me feel more like myself or less?

If your crew can't celebrate your growth without feeling threatened, it's time to clean house.

Four Types of People to Let Go Of

Let's name names — not actual people, but archetypes.

These are the folks who quietly corrode your confidence and keep you stuck. They claim to want what's best for you, but they drain your energy from the inside out.

1. The Graveyard Cheerleader

He's the friend who laughs when you self-sabotage.

He invites you out for drinks when you say you're trying to cut back.

He excuses the shitty things you do to others and yourself.
This guy isn't helping.
He's handing you the shovel to dig your own grave.
You need boundaries, and if he can't accept you've outgrown the version of yourself he was comfortable with, kick his ass to the curb.

2. The Energy Vampire

You feel drained five minutes after they walk in.
Every conversation centers on their problems.
Every topic turns into a rant.
Every interaction is a fire for you to put out.
It's not just that they're struggling; it's that they feed off struggle.
And your loyalty to them is costing you your peace.

3. The Main Character

Life is their movie, and you're just an unpaid extra.
This person only loves you when you're emotionally, financially, and socially beneath them.
They like you most when you're at your lowest. Because the second you stand too tall, they start pulling away, or worse, making little digs to cut you down.
That's not friendship. That's sabotage.
Every activity, every conversation — even your problems — somehow becomes about them.

4. The Bad Influence

Like the Graveyard Cheerleader, the Bad Influence actively tries to pull you back into a version of yourself you've outgrown. But this doesn't just grab his popcorn and watch the carnage; he's right beside you every step of the way.

One of the hardest decisions I've ever made was stepping away from a close friend who'd become a bad influence. We'd grown up together, sharing years of shared laughs, struggles, and inside jokes, but none of that outweighed the fact that I could no longer be the man I'd grown into and still be his friend.

We were both married at the time. He cheated on his wife constantly and mocked me because I wasn't interested in joining his sex crusades.

"You're being a pussy," he told me more than once, just because I chose to go home to my wife and kid.

When he asked me to lie for him — to flat-out lie to his wife — and I refused, he questioned my loyalty. He couldn't grasp that I didn't sign up to be his co-conspirator. I wasn't willing to become collateral damage in his self-destruction.

Real men are honest with their wives. Real friends don't ask you to lie to yours — or theirs.

When his wife found out and the fallout hit, he leaned on me hard and expected me to help pick up the pieces. But he didn't want my opinion when the dust settled and he was ready to cheat again.

He wanted a wingman, not a friend.

My then-wife didn't want me hanging out with him anymore; neither did I.

Spend enough time surrounded by shit, and you'll start to smell like it.

We've all had a friend like that — the one who ignores your boundaries, tries to pressure you into situations you'll regret, and doesn't give a damn about the consequences you'll face because of their actions.

That's not friendship. That's manipulation.

You can't live clean with friends who try pulling you into the mud.

Love them from a distance if you must. But let them go.

You don't need a dramatic exit. Sometimes, you just stop picking up the phone.

The only way to replace dead weight is to surround yourself with people who actually give a damn about you — and themselves.

Men Need Men Who Give a Damn

We don't talk enough about how many men struggle to form genuine male friendships.

Not drinking buddies.

Not trash-talk partners.

Not the "hit me up when you're in town" types.

I mean real, solid, brother-level friendships.

Men who:

- Let you be vulnerable without using it against you.
- Talk about more than sports, sex, or work.
- Call you out with love.
- Celebrate your wins instead of competing with you.
- Want to grow with you, not just age beside you.

But we weren't raised for that.

Most of us were taught that male bonding means sarcasm, insults, and pretending nothing ever bothers you.

That kind of "friendship" doesn't build confidence; it buries it.

You don't need a wolf pack.

You need a tribe: a crew of men with integrity, emotional intelligence, and the guts to push you toward your potential.

Leveling Up the Circle

So, how do you find these men?

How do you build a better circle?

You become the kind of man better men are drawn to.

No one wants to have a deep, grounded conversation with a guy who's still performing, lying to himself, or clinging to victimhood.

But when you...

- live your values (even when it's more difficult),
- speak directly and honestly (without being a dick),
- own your emotions (without making them everyone else's

problem),

- set boundaries (without guilt), and
- give (without expecting anything back)

…you become magnetic to people who are also walking that path.

They won't be perfect. But they'll be intentional.

They'll grow with you, challenge you, and catch you when needed.

And you'll show up for them the same way.

When your circle is strong, you stop second-guessing yourself, defending your worth, or performing to be accepted.

You show up honest, grounded, and clear.

And the right people meet you there — not because you shrink to fit, but because they value the full, unapologetic, high-integrity version of you.

That's when everything about you shifts: your walk, your tone, your presence.

That's when your confidence takes root.

Your Turn: Inner Circle Audit

Grab a piece of paper or open your Notes app. List the five people you spend the most time with (virtually or in real life).

Then ask yourself:

1. Do I feel energized or drained after spending time with them?

2. Do they challenge me to grow or help me stay stuck?

3. Can I be my true self with them, or am I always performing?

If someone regularly makes you feel smaller, unseen, or like you're not allowed to be you, that relationship needs to change.

Set a boundary. Limit their access. And if needed, walk away.

And if your list gets short?

Good. That means you're finally choosing quality over quantity, and that's how you start leveling up.

Matt Murphy

Chapter Thirteen
Embracing the Awkwardness

Most of us men are terrified of looking awkward.

We'll dodge singing, dancing, trying new shit, speaking up, or asking for help to avoid looking like dumbasses. God forbid someone catch us vulnerable — or worse, showing that we don't know what we're doing.

Here's the truth:

Every ounce of confidence you're chasing is hiding behind awkwardness. That uncomfortable feeling? It's not a red light; it's a green one. It means you've stepped into growth territory. And that's exactly where Big Dick Energy gets forged.

Awkwardness Is a Training Ground

Awkwardness isn't your enemy. It's your gym. It's where confidence gets beaten up, rebuilt, and made stronger.

- The first time you speak in public? Awkward.
- The first time you set a boundary with a parent? Awkward.

- The first time you fart in front of your lover? Awkward as hell — especially when it surprises you both.

Each time you do it, you send a message to yourself:

"I'm allowed to feel awkward. But I'm not letting that shit stop me."

And that message is rocket fuel for confidence.

What Avoiding Awkward Costs You

Most men believe that moments of awkwardness make them appear weak. In reality, avoiding awkwardness often makes them look guarded, boring, or emotionally constipated.

Discomfort and vulnerability are frequent landmarks of the road to Big Dick Energy, where there are no shortcuts.

Here's what you lose when you dodge awkwardness:

- People you never meet
- New skills and hobbies you never discover
- Depth you never gain
- Growth that never happens

You can't become someone new without letting go of who you were; the gap between those two versions is always uncomfortable.

But you've got to be willing to look a little dumb if you ever want to become someone who doesn't give a damn about looking dumb.

Confidence Is the Willingness to Look Stupid (For a While)

Want confidence singing karaoke? You'll probably bomb a few songs first.

Want confidence in relationships? You've got to say something real — and risk getting shot down.

Want confidence in your body? Show up to the gym, the class, or the beach looking like a work in progress (because you are).

That's the entry fee. Most never pay it. That's why most stay stuck.

But if you're still reading this? You might be ready.

Field Trip: The Line-Dancing Bar

A line-dancing floor is one of the best places to see awkwardness transform into confidence in real time.

You don't have to throw on boots and hit the nearest honkytonk for this one. If beer and cowboy hats aren't your thing, fair enough. But if you want a front-row seat to courage turning into growth, go see it for yourself.

At any moment, you'll see all skill levels out there: some look like pros, mixing in their own moves, others stumble along, copying the person in front of them. But the newbies? They're not just tolerated — they're welcomed. Because every seasoned dancer remembers what it's like to feel lost and clumsy, hoping the next quarter-turn doesn't land them front and center with no one to follow.

Here's the beauty of it: every song has its own choreography. Even the best dancers have to learn new steps when a fresh one drops. But they've trained their confidence. They're cool with looking like newbs until they've got it down.

Pro tip, fellas: you won't be hurting for attention from the ladies if you get your ass out there and give it a shot.

Perseverance Through Discomfort is Magnetic

Nobody's impressed by perfection.

What really draws people in? Authenticity — especially when you're real under pressure.

The guy who screws up and laughs at himself is magnetic.

The guy who trips over his words during a speech but keeps going is powerful.

The guy who says, "I'm not good at this yet, but I'm here, and I'm trying," is a man showing Big Dick Energy.

Owning your awkward moments sends a powerful message:

"I'm secure enough to be vulnerable."

Your Turn: Choose Awkward on Purpose

Here's your homework. Pick one awkward thing and do it this week. Seriously.

- Sign up for a class and try something new.
- Talk to a stranger. Yes, simply start a conversation. It's legal in most states.
- Sing karaoke.
- Tell someone you admire them, even if it makes you sweat.
- Admit you're clueless about something.

Don't overthink it afterward.
Don't pick apart how dumb you think you looked.
Celebrate the fact that you showed up.
That's the win. That's the rep. That's how your confidence muscles grow.

Karaoke: The Cheat Code

My mom ran a karaoke business for nearly twenty years before she passed in 2014. Every time I visited home, she'd ask me to sing at one of her gigs, and aside from a couple of drunken nights I barely remember, I always said no.

The thought of singing in public felt perversely vulnerable, like bending over and spreading my ass cheeks in front of a crowd. (And just like that scenario, it only happened a couple of drunken nights I barely remember.)

You know how your music dips when the GPS gives directions? That volume drop was enough to embarrass me if I was singing in the car — even alone!

Last fall, Shara and I were on a cruise and ended up at the karaoke bar. A couple teased each other in front of us, both trying to talk the other into singing.

"I'd do 'Rapper's Delight,' but I don't have anyone to sing it with me," the guy said.

"It would be so hot if you got up there and sang," Shara whispered. And she can convince me to do almost anything by starting a sentence with, "It would be so hot if…"

Fuck it. I nudged the man and said, "I've got you. Let's do this." I cringed when I heard myself say the words; I blame the cocktails.

Neither of us was the next Wonder Mike. Still, we rapped our hearts out, got asses moving on the dance floor, and even earned a few of those rare "OK, I see you" comments that black people affectionately say to white people who unexpectedly pull off something considered "black."

Two weeks after we returned from the cruise, we hit a local dive bar on a Wednesday, unaware that it was karaoke night.

The DJ, Jason, came over and asked if we wanted to sing.

Shara said, "I don't sing, but I'm a great cheerleader."

Singing on a cruise in front of a bunch of people I'd never see again was one thing; this bar was three miles from my house. "If I'm drunk enough to sing, it's time to cut me off," I laughed.

Then I saw Shara's shoulders slump. And look — when you've got a great woman, you do what it takes to make her smile.

"Fine," I said. "Put my name on the list."

Not only was I about to sing karaoke, I was cannonballing straight into the deep end. The first round was Kamikaze Karaoke: you draw a random song from a bucket and sing it for a free drink.

Luckily, I knew the song I pulled: "Song of the South" by Alabama.

And I killed it.

OK, "killed it" might be generous. I sang it well enough that nobody cringed, and I didn't embarrass myself. On a normal scorecard, maybe a five out of ten. But for a newbie pulling a random song from a bucket in his local bar? Fucking ten out of ten.

Two things happened: karaoke became one of our go-to nights out, and the local karaoke crew welcomed us in.

That first night, people kept coming up to chat. I laughed to myself; I'd been to that bar fifty times as a single guy, and the only one I ever talked to was the bartender.

Karaoke broke the ice better than yelling, "Drinks are on me!" on a Saturday night.

Fellas, karaoke is a goddamn social cheat code.

Want to meet people? That's how you do it.

Yeah, you might bomb. But you'll earn your place in the fraternity of guys and gals with the balls to try.

Nobody cares if you're not a great singer. But if you get up there just to bomb on purpose, the room will turn on you quickly. Squawking your way through "Don't Stop Believing" like a pissed-off crow isn't Big Dick Energy; it's insecurity disguised as self-deprecation theater.

Try and fail? That's fine. But don't waste everyone's time. Either go for it or stay in your seat.

Now that I've stepped outside my karaoke comfort zone, I push myself to sing at least one new song every time we go out.

Sometimes, I bomb, but I'd rather flop than play it safe and grow complacent.

It's important to give yourself a break when stepping out of your comfort zone. Equally important is giving grace to others who are facing awkward situations.

I don't care if you sing like Frank Sinatra — if you're mocking someone for trying, whether it's singing, dancing, or just showing up vulnerable, then you suck at karaoke — and at life.

They Call Him Batman

There's this long-haired guy in the local karaoke crowd everyone calls "Batman." He's pushing sixty, sings his ass off, hypes up every performer no matter their skill level, and always shows up with a smile, a kind word, and zero fucks to give. Everyone loves him.

I've met few men more at ease in their own skin. He rocks long socks under combat boots, black shorts, and a rotating lineup of Batman T-shirts — every karaoke night, even in winter. Why? Because it's what he likes. He's not waiting for anyone's permission to be himself.

Shara and I went to a Fourth of July party at his place last month. There had to be a hundred people there; they were his *friends*, not party crashers. And that was just those who didn't already have plans. Genuine, kind people are magnetic as fuck.

If I threw a party, I'm not sure I could get twenty people to show up with a month's notice. That's something I hope to change.

Batman embodies Big Dick Energy. And it's refreshing to see someone living it out loud in my backyard.

Big Dick Energy Grows in Awkward Moments

Confidence isn't about being smooth.

It means you show up anyway, knowing you might trip over your own feet — and do it with a wink and a smile.

When you embrace the awkwardness and get comfortable facing the uncomfortable, you silence your voice of self-doubt.

You allow yourself to be human.

And you give that same permission to everyone around you.

That's not just confidence. That's inspiration.

So, sing the karaoke song or take the dance class. Do the thing that makes your palms sweat — and hype up anyone else doing the same.

You don't get BDE by dodging the awkward — you get it by showing up, screwing up, and coming back for more.

Chapter Fourteen: Your Dick

Speaking of awkward, let's talk about your dick like grown men.

Not metaphorically. Not spiritually. I mean your actual, physical penis — the one you probably started obsessing about somewhere between age nine and your first gym-class shower.

It's time we lay it out (pun intended) and talk about one of the most misunderstood and anxiety-inducing topics in modern masculinity: penis size.

The Biggest Lie You've Been Told

Somewhere along the way, we started believing that being manly was directly proportional to the length of the tube hanging between our legs.

That bigger equals better.

That size equals status.

Do you know where this came from?

The obsession came from men, not women.

Porn. Locker-room talk. Insecure boys bragging. And decades of media that equated sexual prowess with something you have no control over.

Let's be clear: porn isn't inherently evil, but it's not a blueprint for real sex. It's a performance; it's shot for angles, exaggeration, and clicks. The average male porn star has an above-average member, but that's exactly why they're in porn. Feeling inadequate because you're not hung like a porn star is like feeling bad about your jump shot after watching an NBA game.

The problem is that too many men carry that performance anxiety into real life. They see their average size — because yes, most men are average — and feel ashamed. Or worse, they internalize the belief that they're a lesser man because they weren't born with a novelty-sized phallus.

That's not just sad. It's self-sabotage.

Let's address another myth while we're at it: that all women are size queens who only want huge dicks.

Some do. Some don't. Just like some guys love huge boobs and others don't care. It's a preference, not a universal truth.

But you know what women almost universally value in bed?

Confidence.

Attunement.

Generosity.

Passion.

Presence.

The ability to make them feel safe enough to let go fully.

If you're lying there overthinking your size like it's the opening line on your résumé, you're not present in the moment. You're with your insecurities, not with her.

And she can feel that.

Here's the deal: if you're obsessed with your dick, she will be too — but not in the way you want. She'll sense your shame, need for validation, tension, and desperation to prove something. And nothing is less sexy than a man trying to prove something he doesn't need to.

Insecurity Is the Real Turnoff

Men with smaller dicks who approach romance and intimacy with shame and defensiveness reinforce the bullshit belief that size is what matters. It's a self-fulfilling prophecy.

While I was on dating apps, I noticed many women's profiles had specific height requirements — and some of those women were even short. Though I'm nearly six feet tall, I found their "must be this tall to ride" policy interesting. I asked some of them why height mattered so much. A few said they didn't want to tower over their date in heels, but more said they'd had bad experiences with insecure short men.

The same can be said for men obsessed with their dick size.

If you act like it's a problem, you're saying, "This *is* something to be ashamed of." And that mindset doesn't just ruin your sex life; it bleeds into your self-image, your confidence, and your relationships.

It's not a small dick that turns women away — it's Small Dick Energy.

A man with a smaller dick who moves through life and loves with power, presence, and confidence will always outshine a man with a horse cock and the emotional maturity of a teenager.

Do you know what Big Dick Energy *really* is? It's a man who knows and owns who he is (and what he's packing).

Let's Talk Science

When your partner says your dick size is fine, believe her. Sure, some assholes might say it was tiny after a breakup, but if it wasn't a communicated problem during your relationship, it was never a problem.

The science backs it up.

In 2006, researchers J. Lever, D. Frederick, and L. Peplau surveyed 52,000 people. They found that 85% of women were satisfied with their partner's penis size. Only 55% of men were satisfied with their own. That's nearly half of men and only 3 in 20 women who are dissatisfied. What the fuck are we doing here, guys?

How exhausting would it be if women obsessed over the idea that men only liked boobs with perfectly symmetrical nipples — and wouldn't believe us, no matter how many times 85% of us told them it didn't matter?

Of course, I also did my own totally unscientific research at a local bar. Here's what three women had to say when I asked about dick size (and yes, I knew them well enough to ask):

Lady #1: "I've only remembered dick size three times — twice because they were too big and once because it was smaller than my pinky. Guys worry about that shit way more than women."

Lady #2: "If it's above average, it's not going inside me. I don't want my cervix shoved into my lungs."

Lady #3: "Will you fucking move, dude? I'm trying to shoot pool."

Learn How to Use the Tools You Have

Statistically speaking, your penis size is probably average. But let's say your dick is on the smaller side. So what?

You still have:

- Hands and mouth
- Toys and creativity
- Timing and rhythm
- Communication skills and emotional connection
- Chris Stapleton on your playlist

Sex isn't a demolition derby; it's an experience. And most women orgasm through clitoral stimulation, not penetration. If you don't know that (or don't care to learn it), that's not a dick problem. That's a you problem.

If you're still operating under the belief that your penis is the sole driver of pleasure, you're not just missing the point; you're letting every partner you've ever had down.

Fix Your Beliefs, Not Your Body

Let's say science offered you a guaranteed penis-enlargement procedure tomorrow with no side effects. Would you feel better?

Maybe. But only if your problem was really about size.

That's not usually the issue. It's about feeling inadequate. You feel small, so you obsess over something measurable.

Confidence isn't measured by inches.

You don't need a bigger dick. You need a better mindset.

You need to see your body as a powerful instrument — not in comparison to others, but in its ability to love, feel, move, connect, and pleasure.

Your Dick Doesn't Define You

Your kindness does. Your presence does. Your truth-telling, emotional availability, consistency, and courage do.

Big Dick Energy beats a big dick damn near every time.

Most men who radiate confidence don't have six-pack abs or eight-inch dicks. They just have nothing to prove.

So the next time you catch yourself wondering whether you measure up, remember:

Big Dick Energy isn't about what's in your jeans — or genes. It's about what's in your *presence*.

Own your presence, and you'll never measure yourself in inches again.

Chapter Fifteen
Love Like a Man with BDE

After Laura (the nurse) dumped me and I returned to the dating apps in the spring of 2023, I quickly grew exhausted from the whole routine: matching, fishing for talking points, and hoping that mutual curiosity would graduate to interest.

I got a Like on Tinder in early June from a cute blonde named Shara. She was 39, and her profile said she was still figuring out what she was looking for. Her interests included dogs and country music. She looked good in her photos, and we shared some common interests, so I swiped right.

We connected instantly, talking about our dogs and outlaw country, and soon moved the conversation to text. From the start, I was more interested than usual. But my interest skyrocketed when we, two people who hated talking on the phone, had our first phone conversation.

Shara had an abrasive charm. She'd drawn a line in the sand after taking shit from a coward for years, and once she found the courage to leave him, she wasn't about to start that cycle again. She wasn't looking for a relationship; she planned to date casually for the first time.

A self-described Mississippi hick who'd transformed into a Florida woman, Shara acted accordingly: paddle-boarding in the springs on the weekends, arguing with me that Willie Nelson was better than Merle Haggard, and teasing me about driving a hybrid.

We spent hours on the phone, losing track of time and sacrificing sleep just to talk a little longer. I was so captivated before our first date that I didn't even care what Shara looked like in person. She was awesome, and even if there wasn't a romantic spark, I still wanted to be her friend.

I was in for a pleasant surprise.

When we finally met a week later, I was stunned. Shara's profile pictures hadn't done her justice; she'd *reverse*-catfished me! She was beautiful — long blonde hair, magnetic blue eyes, and an ornery smile. She was out of my lea—

Nope!

I wasn't falling into my old way of thinking.

Maybe it was the way we'd connected over the phone, or maybe it was the way her small dress showcased a jaw-dropping figure that short-circuited my brain, but I kissed her before I even said hello. Not typical start-of-the-first-date behavior for me.

We had one hell of a first date, starting with beers at a brewery, moving to dinner at a nearby restaurant, and ending with a romantic, hand-in-hand walk through the park.

Over the next few weeks, she tried to warn me that she'd hurt me ("Hurt people *hurt* people," they say) and doubted her capacity to love. But I could tell by the way she loved Atlas, her Golden Retriever who warmed up to me right away and soon stole my heart, that she loved deeply.

Despite our efforts to tamp down the groundswell of desire, we were in an exclusive relationship within a month.

In a world of filters, fillers, and fakery, she was real. She was present in the moment, often forgetting her phone even had a camera, let alone stopping to create content for social media. Blue-collar tough, white-collar smart, and as unwilling as I was to wear a mask for anyone, she was a breath of fresh air.

The moment I knew I'd fallen in love, I decided I was going to get this one right. If anyone had earned my best, it was her. I've kept that energy ever since, and she's proven every day that she's worth it.

Two years into our relationship, I'm happier than I've ever been. We're best friends, and I've missed more than a few exits from getting so wrapped up in our conversations while I drive. A lifelong junkie for solitude, I've never once wished she weren't there, and I miss her when she's not. We lean on each other when we need support and nudge each other when we need motivation.

I'd lived in Florida for four years before we met, but I'd never truly lived the Florida experience. Shara brought out the Florida man in me: she introduced me to kayaking in the springs, walking on the beach, eating boiled peanuts, and hitting festivals. I still don't know if I love doing those things or just doing them with her, but I get excited for every new adventure. Florida has become more than the setting for our love story; it's become its own character.

Shara and I rarely argue, but when we do, our arguments are solution-oriented and grounded in love. We put "us" before ourselves, and whatever ego either of us has left doesn't creep into our debates.

> *"It is better to lose your pride with someone you love*
> *rather than to lose that someone you love with your useless pride."*
> —John Ruskin

For the first time in my life, I'm loving — and being loved — in a healthy, sustainable way. I can see in her eyes how deeply she loves me and that I'm loving her right.

And that I finally achieved a Big Dick Energy that doesn't go soft.

"How did *you* end up with *her*?"

A guy asked me that while we were both pissing onto pink urinal cakes in a bar bathroom — separate urinals, of course. I didn't blame him; Shara turns heads when we go out, and I probably look like the dude who installed your Internet. Weird place for the conversation, though.

"I hit the jackpot when I got her," I said. "And I work hard to keep deserving her."

But this wasn't just about landing a great woman; it was about finally loving from a place of real confidence. And that changed everything.

At another local bar, a regular named Ashley approached me while Shara stepped away to the restroom.

"She's so gorgeous," she said.

"Thanks," I replied. "I agree."

"No offense, but when I first saw you two together, I wondered how you got her. But I've been watching the way you treat her and the way you carry yourself — and now it makes sense. You've got that Big Dick Energy."

And just like that, my writer's block was gone.

(Thanks, Ashley!)

Here's what my relationship with Shara has taught me about Big Dick Energy:

- It doesn't disappear when you fall in love; it's not something you take off at the door like muddy boots.
- When you learn to love yourself and have healthy masculine confidence, it's easy to love someone else the right way.
- Real love will amplify your confidence, not erode it.

But most men don't know how to carry confidence into a relationship.

They shrink to avoid conflict, dominate to avoid vulnerability, perform to stay liked, or detach the moment things get real.

That's not love.

That's insecurity.

Loving with strength, presence, humility, and authenticity is loving like a man with Big Dick Energy.

BDE in Love Means You're Not Needy, You're Available

Here's the difference.

A needy man says:

"I need you to complete me."
"I need you to make me feel worthy."
"If you leave, I'll fall apart."

An emotionally available man says:
"I hear you."
"I'm with you because I want you."
"I'm open, honest, present, and invested, but I won't vanish if you don't approve of every part of me."

One is rooted in fear and insecurity.
The other is rooted in confidence and self-worth.

Big Dick Energy in relationships means you're whole already. You're not seeking someone to fix you; you're inviting someone to grow with you.

You Don't Have to Be "The Man" to Be a Good Partner

There's an outdated idea that men in relationships must lead, dominate, provide, protect, solve every problem, and never show fear. That version of masculinity is exhausting.

You don't have to be "The Man" in a relationship. You just have to be a man worth being with.

That means:
You can express your emotions without shame.
You can ask for help or space without guilt.
You don't need to control every outcome.
You can apologize without falling apart.
You can fall apart without apologizing.

Strong men take responsibility without taking over. And it's a great feeling to be in a collaborative relationship where you can trust your partner to take the reins, too.

Radical Honesty

Shara would probably blaspheme the sacred name of Willie Nelson before she'd ever create content; her disdain for social media is one of her many charms. Still, I wish I could live-stream the rare occasion we disagree. We attack problems, not each other. We're calm, patient, and radically honest.

Radical honesty is a level of openness most people never reach with themselves — let alone with a partner.
What is it?
- It's her waking up and telling me she had a dream that I cheated on her and needs to talk through the jealousy she feels, even if she knows it's irrational.
- It's me telling her I did a half-load of laundry because taco night did a number on my boxer briefs.
- It's her telling me that MacGruber was the worst movie she'd ever seen after I was so excited to share it with her.
- It's us speaking without shame about our traumas and anxieties.
- It's us checking in without blame when either of us hits a valley in sex drive.

It only thrives in a space that's free of ego and judgment.
That should be the goal of every healthy relationship.

Most couples aren't more honest than when the relationship is ending. The moment someone calls it quits, the cork pops off all those bottled-up feelings, and the truth sprays out like someone just won the World Series. I'm not talking about childish insults like "You have a tiny dick" or "You should do something about your feminine odor," but real stuff, like emotional needs that you neglected or she never said aloud.

Why wait until doomsday to speak the truth? Imagine how great a relationship could be if both people were radically honest from the beginning.

The Emotional Cuddle-Blumpkin

I don't spend much time on social media, but I follow an excellent Facebook page called Humans of New York. In May 2023, a month before I met Shara, I read this post on HoNY (used with permission from page owner Brandon Stanton):

Right after we met, I was in the bathroom taking a shit, and she came in and sat on my lap. I was like, No fucking way. That's when I knew she was the one.

Below it was a happy-looking couple embracing.

The post tickled my brain for weeks. Across two marriages, totaling eighteen years, I never once even shared the bathroom while taking a piss. And this brand-new couple was doing a cuddle-blumpkin?

What the fuck? Was this real life? Was that even allowed?

Although I knew I never wanted a lap-cuddle while I was shitting, I couldn't get the post out of my head: I craved that kind of raw connection with someone. I'd never been so open with a romantic partner.

Thanks to our master bathroom's arched doorway with no door, Shara and I got past the bathroom barrier quickly. One of us still leaves the room when the other needs to "do more," but we've had full conversations (with eye contact!) while the other pees.

I don't know what my hang-up was about peeing in front of someone — I'm not shy about farts — but I'm relieved (see what I did there?) we didn't waste time getting over that hump.

Neither Shara nor I have sat on each other's lap during a shit, and we don't plan to change that. Still, we cuddle-blumpkin each other emotionally, embracing and sharing without shame, even when we're at our most vulnerable. I never knew humans could connect so closely, and if I died tomorrow, I'm happy I've had a chance to experience it.

It might have never happened if it weren't for that HoNY post.

Radical honesty is about being emotionally naked in everyday moments.

Follow the Blueprint

Have you ever been blindsided by a break-up? You think things are going great, and then she abruptly ends it for no apparent reason?

It happens to most of us.

While some women dump guys because they're bored or someone else has caught their eye, few go through the drama of a break-up for no reason. Often, it's because they don't feel heard.

When a lady shares her needs — especially the emotional ones — she's giving her man the blueprint to keep her.

How many times did she say things like this without seeing results?

- "I could use some cuddle time tonight."
- "Can you put your controller down for a few minutes so we can chat?"
- "I'm tired from my workday, too. But we still need to work together to keep the house clean."

Blindsided? No apparent reason? Maybe, but not usually.

BDE Knows When to Stay and When to Walk

A confident man doesn't stay in a relationship out of fear.

He also doesn't run just because it gets hard.

He chooses her consciously. Intentionally.

He stays when it's worth growing through.

He walks when he's being disrespected, devalued, or emotionally starved.

Big Dick Energy doesn't manipulate, beg, or chase.

It speaks clearly, sets boundaries, and knows it's worthy of a love rooted in emotional intimacy.

Emotional Intimacy Is the Ultimate Flex

Let me be blunt. If you can't have hard emotional conversations, you're not ready for intimacy. You can be great in bed and say all the right things. But if you check out the moment someone cries, criticizes you, or shows their messy side, you're still playing dress-up.

Big Dick Energy holds steady during hard times.

- It listens without defensiveness.
- It speaks without blame.
- It sits in discomfort without running.

You can't have intimacy without honesty. Period. Sure, you can insert your penis and gyrate to and fro, but that's not intimacy. Intimacy isn't just skin on skin; it's shared truth, even when that truth is messy, embarrassing, or unexpected. When you lie (by omission or commission), you build walls where there should be bridges. Real connection requires vulnerability, and vulnerability is impossible without honesty.

If you're hiding key parts of yourself, you're not being loved; you're managing a performance. That's public relations work, not intimacy.

And never does honesty pay off more than when you're talking about what happens in the bedroom.

Let's Talk About Sex

If you want to feel emotionally safe, you've got to speak openly about sex. Because intimacy isn't just physical — it's psychological.

Too many men go years — even lifetimes — without telling a partner what really turns them on. They're afraid of being judged, rejected, or laughed at, and terrified she will share his secret with her friends. So they play it safe. But suppressing your kinks doesn't make you more desirable; it makes you resentful, distant, and unfulfilled. A healthy sexual relationship requires communication, not choreography. You can't expect your partner to meet your needs if you're too ashamed to name them.

Want to role-play or watch porn together?
Tell her.

Curious about something kinkier, like a finger in your butt?
Tell her.

Want to start visiting swingers' clubs together?
Maybe tread lightly on that one.

You have to communicate. Get as comfortable talking about intimacy and sex as you are talking about your day at work.

Don't just share: create a space where your partner feels safe to share, too. Listen attentively with your ears and mind open. You can't mock your partner's fantasies and then complain that she's stopped communicating her desires.

Being honest about your desires isn't just about getting your needs met; it's how you demonstrate emotional safety to each other.

If you can't be honest with the person you're naked with, where can you be?

Sharing your kinks doesn't mean you have to act on all of them. It means you trust someone enough to bring your full self to the table. That kind of transparency builds trust — and trust is the foundation of intimacy.

Want a more adventurous, more connected, more satisfying sex life? Start by being honest — not just about what you want, but about who you are.

That's when you'll find real connection.

Because real love requires real presence, not perfect words or a flawless image.

Speaking of honesty in the bedroom, let's talk about the kind of awkward moment most guys would rather fake their own death than admit.

The Blue Pill

Emotional intimacy requires openly discussing more than fantasies. Too many bedrooms grow cold because couples don't communicate when things change.

- One partner experiences a dip in libido.
- The old bedroom tricks aren't getting the job done anymore.
- Life stress makes it hard to stay present.

You have to push through the discomfort and have those hard conversations. When you do, you might be surprised how close it brings you. Avoid them, and they'll pull you apart.

Two years ago, I had my first real experience struggling to keep my soldier battle-ready. Sure, I'd had the occasional moment — too drunk, too tired, too distracted — but this happened three times in less than two weeks. I wasn't even 45; I was too young for erectile dysfunction, right?

My younger self would've felt humiliated, maybe even emasculated. But the new, better me didn't flinch. I told Shara (who was supportive and understanding), and I saw a doctor who prescribed Viagra. And holy shit, did it work the first time I took it!

Soon, I learned I didn't need the pill. It wasn't dysfunction, just a temporary dip.

Though I haven't had the issue since, it's nice to know the bottle is still in my medicine cabinet in case my special friend gets lazy again. It's even nicer to know I'm comfortable openly talking about it with my lady.

This isn't an ad for dick pills. It's a case study in the power of honest communication. I didn't sulk or roll away in quiet shame. I spoke up. And that strengthened our trust instead of making her wonder if she'd done something wrong — or if the flame was dying.

There's no better feeling than knowing you're safe to be as

emotionally naked — vulnerable and radically honest — as you are physically.

BDE doesn't fear failure (or a limp noodle). It uses it as an excuse to laugh, connect, and maybe get a prescription... You know, just in case.

You Can Be Sexual and Still Respectful as Hell

BDE in bed is about presence, not performance. It can be filthy and fun, but never careless. It's strong, but never unsafe. It's assertive, but never selfish.

You can be:

- Dominant without being degrading.
- Free without being reckless.
- Passionate without being performative.

There's nothing more attractive to most decent women than a man who is confident in what he wants but attuned enough to ask, listen, and adjust.

If she tells you something smells funky down there, hear her and act accordingly. Hop in the shower (don't forget to wash your taint), then thank her for being honest.

If she asks for more foreplay, give it to her. She's telling you she needs something more. You can either sulk and get defensive, or you can listen and deliver. Sulking and defensiveness build walls; listening and delivering build bridges.

Some women find penetration most enjoyable when they're on top. If your lady tells you that, believe her. Check your ego — even if you think you've got moves like Jagger. You'd rather be a pillow prince with a satisfied partner than a sex machine only pleasing your hand, wouldn't you? You can always make up the cardio on the treadmill.

Big Dick Energy is sexy because it feels safe.
Not boring — safe. The "I can fully be myself with this per-

son" kind of safe.

That's the intimacy most people crave.

Your Turn: Show Up with Big Dick Energy in Love

If you have a partner, try this:

1. Initiate a hard conversation with no ducking or deflecting.

Ask them what they wish you'd do differently in the relationship. Don't defend. Just listen.

2. Compliment like a man who notices more than her curves.

Not just "you're hot." Try something that acknowledges her growth journey, not just her ass. "I appreciate you making me feel heard during our disagreement last night." Let her feel seen.

3. Admit something uncomfortable.

A fear, a mistake, a need — speak it out loud. Watch what it does to the emotional depth between you.

4. Set a boundary lovingly.

Respect yourself enough to say, "This doesn't work for me," without anger or drama.

Love Like You Deserve It

Here's the bottom line:

You don't have to be perfect to be worthy of love.

You have to be present, honest, and fully yourself.

That's how a man with Big Dick Energy loves.

That's the kind of love worth keeping — and the kind a stranger might ask you about at the urinal.

Matt Murphy

Chapter Sixteen
When Shit Still Goes Sideways

I'd rebuilt myself. I was living and loving with Big Dick Energy. But all the BDE in the world won't keep life from kicking you squarely in the balls.

While soul-searching, I made important decisions about who — and what — I would tolerate in my life. Unfortunately, that didn't mesh well with my work situation.

I had the kind of job people envied: a high-profile, lucrative role in an exciting field, working for a top-tier company. At one time, the crew felt like a family.

Then, everything changed. The workplace I knew and loved became toxic, and I grew unhappy.

Even if the rest of your life is going well, a toxic job can suck the joy — and the life — out of you.

I knew I was worth betting on, so I went all-in on myself.

I put in my two-week notice and was fired on the spot. Point made.

My finances took a hit, my social circle narrowed, and people in the industry gossiped and speculated, but I never regretted leaving.

Let's make this very clear:
Big Dick Energy doesn't make you invincible.
Confidence won't stop life from kicking your ass.
It won't protect you from heartbreak, failure, loss, rejection, embarrassment, or self-doubt.
But it gives you the tools to respond like a man who doesn't crumble when things go sideways.

Change is inevitable. Big Dick Energy is resilient and adaptable. It stands tall, weathers the shitstorm, brushes itself off, and keeps moving forward.
This book isn't about avoiding the storm.
It's about becoming the guy who can walk through it without losing himself.

Even the Most Confident Men Get Wrecked Sometimes

You might lose your job.
You might get ghosted.
You might say the wrong thing and catch the wrath of a mob of self-loathing internet weaklings who only feel powerful when they attack *en masse.*
You might watch someone you love hurt — and not know how to fix it.

The question isn't, "Will life kick me in the nuts?"
It's, "Who am I when it does?"

Real BDE Knows How to Fall Without Folding

When I say "fall," I mean those gut-punch moments:
Your wife asks for a divorce.
You get fired.
Your physical or mental health unravels.

Here's what a man with Big Dick Energy does in those moments:

- He acknowledges the pain.
- He reflects on the factors that caused the pain, including his own actions or inactions, and owns it.
- He works through it, learns from it, and slowly rebuilds.

That's what real strength looks like.

It also looks like:
Apologizing to your wife, even after there's no saving the marriage.
Taking a lower-level position while you reroute your career.
Scheduling a therapy appointment without shame.

Getting back up isn't about grit; it's about capacity. That kind of internal strength that gets built long before the fall. When life kicks your ass, it's not raw willpower that lifts you. It's the foundation you've built that strengthens your core.

The Capacity to Weather the Storm

You can't control the weather. Some things are just out of your hands.
But you can build the capacity to endure the storms.

Your capacity is:

Emotional range — the scope and intensity of feelings you can experience and express.
Resilience — the ability to recover, to bend without breaking.
Adaptability — the flexibility to adjust to change.
Restraint — the discipline to act intentionally instead of reacting emotionally.
Patience — the calm to wait for planted seeds to grow.
Confidence — the trust that you're equipped to face whatever comes.

Sometimes, capacity means getting caught in a violent hailstorm, covering your head with a trash can lid, and riding it out.

Sometimes, there is no lid, and all you can do is brace for each frozen nugget that smacks your skull.

Whether or not you're religious, the Serenity Prayer still holds value:

> *God, grant me the serenity*
> *to accept the things I cannot change,*
> *the courage to change the things I can,*
> *and the wisdom to know the difference.*

The Weak Hate Setbacks. The Strong Learn from Them.

A weak man says:
"I can't take this."
"Why is this always happening to me?"
"I'm a failure."

A strong man says:
"I didn't want this, but I can handle it."
"What can I do to keep this from happening again?"
"How can I grow something useful from underneath this pile of shit?"

The moment you stop seeing failure as proof you're unworthy and start seeing it as part of your growth journey is when you begin adding the depth of wisdom to your confidence.

Your Turn: Build a Storm Protocol

We men like to think of ourselves as protectors, but many of us neglect preparing for emergencies. We assume we'll have the right answer or tool for anything life throws at us. But that's not reality. Preparation is power.

Every man should have emergency plans in place for severe weather and other emergencies.

I live in Florida, hurricane territory. Last year, Hurricane Helene narrowly missed us, but Milton didn't. The storm knocked out power for days. Grocery stores were closed. No running water, no internet. A tornado snapped trees in both yards next to mine. I'd lived in Florida for five years, and it was the first time a hurricane did more than inconvenience me.

We were mostly ready, but the storm revealed some holes in our emergency plan.

Now, we keep a few cases of bottled water stashed away; the store shelves will be empty. We know alternate routes to the highway in case downed trees block the roads. We've got an emergency weather radio.

You need the same kind of emergency plan — for your emotions.

Here's how to start your emotional storm plan:

1. Know who you'll call.

Pick one person who gets the unfiltered version of you and gives you theirs in return. Someone who won't flinch when you're messy, and won't bullshit you when you need truth. Tell them what happened.

Important: This is not a job for social media. You need an actual human, not a few digital hugs from people who'll forget about you five seconds later when the algorithm feeds them a cute puppy video.

2. Silence the noise.

Unplug. Get off social media. Turn off the news. Avoid drama queens and energy vampires. You're in crisis mode — spare no fucks for distractions. Guard your peace like it's your job.

3. Have a ritual that grounds you.

Walk. Journal. Meditate. Blast music and take a drive. Whatever brings you back to center, make it part of your toolkit.

4. Treat your taste buds.

Pick a delicious snack you rarely indulge in — your emergency morale booster. No self-judgment. Just comfort. Mine's a Snickers bar and a Dr. Pepper: 460 empty calories of pure joy.

5. Don't disappear completely.

The world doesn't stop just because you broke down. Give yourself a couple of days off. Cry, sleep, fish, binge through a season of Madden. Then get back to work. Show up. Life still needs you.

5. Pick up the debris and strap on your tool belt.

When the storm clears, repair and rebuild. But keep moving forward. One foot in front of the other, one step at a time, one day at a time — you know the cliches. You've fucking got this!

The Man Who Rises Is the One You Respect

We don't admire men because they've never fallen.

We admire them because they've lost everything and still managed to rebuild.

The ones who broke, grieved, unraveled — and got back up anyway.

That's not weakness. That's strength.

It's not about being unshakable.

It's about knowing that even when the ground splits open beneath you, you've got the fortitude to climb back out.

Life will still go sideways. But you won't.

That's who you've built. That's who you are. And no storm can take that from you.

Chapter Seventeen
Live Like a Man with BDE

If you've made it this far, you've already done something most men never will (and I don't mean finishing a book). You've looked in the mirror, asked the hard questions, and started being honest with yourself.

Now comes the next question:

"Who am I?"

You're not the guy you pretend to be online.

You're not your job title, your relationship status, your bank balance, your body, your dick size, or your worst mistake.

You're the man who's been buried under all that bullshit — and he's been waiting for you to show up.

This Version of You Doesn't Need to Perform

The truest version of you won't be perfect. He won't always say or do the right thing. He won't always know what he's doing.

But he'll show up.

He'll be present.

He'll own his mistakes.

He'll walk away from disrespect.

He'll feel without fear.

And he'll speak the truth.

That's what Big Dick Energy looks like.

Confidence Isn't the Finish Line. It's a Lifestyle.

Here's the truth: you're not "done." You never will be.

Confidence isn't a trophy at the end. It's a muscle you train every day. It's something you build in small, daily decisions that become second nature.

You'll hear, feel, and see the changes in:

- The way you talk to yourself.
- The boundaries you set and enforce.
- The promises you keep.
- The grace you extend.
- The space you create for yourself and others.

You'll still doubt yourself sometimes. You'll still screw up.

But now, you'll own it, learn from it, maybe even laugh at it. Then you'll move forward.

That's how a man with Big Dick Energy lives.

What's Next?

That's up to you.

You can close this book and go back to your default settings.

Nothing changes, but you're one book closer to your Goodreads goal for the year.

Or you can reprogram your default settings from the ground up.

You can become the man who:

- Takes care of himself physically, mentally, and emotionally.
- Commits to ongoing personal growth, even when it's uncomfortable.
- Is a man of his word who says what he means and doesn't seek approval.
- Earns respect and gives it freely.
- Asks for help without shame.
- Cares more about getting it right than being right.
- Takes accountability and apologizes without making excuses.

The man who forgives, embraces the awkward, and leads with honesty — that's the man this book has been building.

That's a man people trust.

That's a man people follow.

That's a man other men respect — and women feel safe with.

That's a man with Big Dick Energy.

A Final Thought (and a Challenge)

If this book hit home, don't just nod and move on.

Do something with it.

- Take one uncomfortable action that aligns with your values.
- Say something hard with respect and clarity.
- Set a boundary you've been avoiding.
- Tell the people you love that you love them. Don't be passive. "Love you" reaches the ears; "I love you" connects with the heart.
- Show up fully. Awkwardly. Honestly. Unapologetically.

And every time you hear the voice of doubt telling you you're not enough, remember this:

Big Dick Energy was never about being the biggest, baddest,

Matt Murphy

or hungest.

It was always about being the most honest, grounded, and real version of yourself.

Now go live like it — and don't you dare go soft.

Live the Movement

This is not the finish line. This is the beginning.

MANifestos is more than a book series. It's a movement to rip off the masks, reject the outdated rules, and rebuild masculinity into something stronger, sharper, and real. It's not about taming men. It's about unmasking them.

Each MANifestos release will be a declaration — raw, unapologetic, and armed with tools to evolve, express, and own your identity in a world that keeps trying to make men either dominate or disappear. We're not interested in either. We're here to build men who show up differently. Authentically.

I chose to self-publish because I'd rather answer to my readers than a publisher. That means I don't have a marketing machine. I have you. If this book hit home, be the reason another man finds it:

Share it in person.

Post it online.

Leave a review on Amazon and Goodreads.

This isn't just my message. It's our movement. And movements live or die based on who carries them forward.

The next chapter of Big Dick Energy isn't written in these pages. It's written in how you live.

Now get out there. Live it. Be it. Pass it on.

Matt Murphy
August 14, 2025
Lake County, Florida

Facebook: MANifestos Media
IG: @manifestosmedia
Reddit: u/manifestosbooks

The 30-Day BDE Challenge

Reclaim your masculinity, one unapologetic day at a time.

Week 1: Know Thyself (Self-Awareness)

1. Mirror Check: Look at yourself in the mirror. Answer the question, "Who am I?" — out loud, if possible.

2. List Your Lies: Write down five lies you tell others (or yourself). Circle the one that's impacting you the most.

3. Own a Flaw: Share a personal insecurity with someone without deflecting or trying to be funny.

4. No Apologies: Go one full day without apologizing for things you don't actually regret.

5. The "Why" Game: Reflect on your last conflict with someone else. Think about what you said or did. Ask yourself, "Why?" until you get to the root of the issue.

6. Confidence Audit: Rate how confident you feel in five areas: career, relationships, appearance, finances, and purpose.

7. Silence the Ego: Catch yourself one time today wanting to impress. Pause. Don't perform. Just exist.

Week 2: Tell the Truth (Honesty & Integrity)

1. Correct One Lie: Come clean about something small you've been hiding.

2. Voice a Boundary: Say "no" to something you'd usually say yes to, just to avoid conflict.

3. Compliment a Man: Say something real and encouraging to another guy without sarcasm or jokes.

4. Kink Check: Write down a sexual desire you've been too afraid to share. Just acknowledge it — for now — without shame.

5. Porn Fast: Take a 48-hour break. Notice your urges. Track your triggers.

6. Tell a Woman the Truth: Say something honest to a woman in your life — loving or difficult, but true.

7. Apologize for Real: Not "I'm sorry *if...*" or "I'm sorry *but...*" Say, "I'm sorry." Period. For the love of bacon, don't say, "I'm sorry you feel that way" when you piss someone off. That's apologizing for their response, not your action.

Week 3: Show Up (Discipline & Presence)

1. Sweat: Do something today that makes your body sweat. Bonus if it hurts a little.

2. Digital Detox: No social media for 24 hours. Use that time to connect IRL (that's "in real life" for you fellow old-timers) with yourself or others.

3. Dress Like You Give a Shit: Wear something that makes you look and feel good, even if you're only going to the store. Put on your "town" clothes, damn it.

4. Do the Hard Thing: Do the thing you've been avoiding.

5. Pay a Debt: Financial, emotional, or relational. Make something right today.

6. Plan a Date: If you're in a relationship, plan and lead a date. If not, plan a solo date. Be present either way — just you and your date (or yourself) in the moment. No phones.

7. Stand Tall: Literally. Shoulders back. Breathe deep. Hold that posture all day. (Repeat every day for the rest of your life.)

Week 4: Big Dick Energy (Courage & Connection)

1. Reclaim a Regret: Write a letter to your younger self. Forgive him.

2. Uplift Without Ulterior Motives: Give a compliment with zero expectations.

3. Ask a Question That Matters: Start a conversation with depth — no sports or no weather.

4. Give Quietly: Do something kind and don't tell a soul.

5. Initiate Sex or Intimacy: With presence. No script. Just honest desire.

6. Burn a Mask: Write down one persona you've been performing. Burn or tear it.

7. Share a Story: Tell someone something you've been through that changed you.

8. Make a Promise: Set one intention for who you want to be.

9. Celebrate Like a Man: No shots, no strippers — unless that's how you roll. Celebrate with something meaningful: a hike, a meal, a call to someone who matters.

Life happens. If you stumble, take a breath, regroup, and try again. Restart the whole damn thing if it helps.

Don't get complacent. Do this challenge a couple of times a year. Change the order each time if you'd like — just don't start with the celebration.

STOP!
Read This Only When You've Finished the 30-Day BDE Challenge!

You didn't wait, did you? (I wouldn't have, either.)

Congrats! You've done it. You've reached... the starting line. Wait. What?

That's right. If you're breathing, you haven't reached the finish line to personal growth. Big Dick Energy requires a focused effort to maintain. Sure, some of the elements become reflexes when you re-program and practice, but you're human, and life is unpredictable. You will lose your footing at times. But you've learned to overcome adversity with confidence.

You've fucking got this!

The Big Dick Energy Manifesto

I pursue authenticity, not approval.
I know who I am, and I don't need to convince them.

I challenge myself.
I call out my own bullshit.

I have the capacity to adapt,
the resilience to persevere, and
the confidence to know I can overcome failure.

I don't measure my worth with dollar signs or tape measures.
My worth is not up for debate.

I set boundaries.
I remove people who don't respect my boundaries.
I remove people who inhibit my growth.

I'm responsible for how I act and react.
I own my shit.

I care deeply, but only about what matters.

I have the balls to speak up,
the wisdom to know when to shut up,
and the presence to show up.

My words are honest.
Those words might offend them.
If I'm wrong, they get an apology.
I don't make excuses.

I pursue continued growth,
but I reject the myth of perfection.

Matt Murphy

I step out of my comfort zone.
I fall on my ass sometimes and laugh at myself.

Other times, life knocks me on my ass.
I always get back up.

My image is what they see.
My character is who I am.
They'll get the real me.
I don't care if they're impressed.

I always command respect.
I never demand respect.
I show them respect and give them trust.
I revoke both if they abuse either.

I don't need to control the narrative.
My truth speaks for itself.
I don't need to win every argument.
I'd rather get it right than be right.

I earned my confidence.
My ego is small.

I build bridges to connect with others.
I don't build walls to keep them out.

I don't shrink to fit in.
I don't inflate to stand out.
I stand tall in exactly who I am.

This is neither ego nor arrogance.
This is confidence and self-awareness.
This is Big Dick Energy.

And I do my best to live it — every damn day.

About the Author

Matt Murphy thinks it's weird writing his own bio in third-person like he's hot shit. But since he's been tasked for this chore, he's going to do it his way.

He's never been the type to sit quietly on the sidelines. A father, two-time divorcee, former pro wrestler, and longtime sports-card breaker, he's lived a life full of comebacks, hard lessons, and second chances. He's been the guy on top, the guy at rock bottom, and the guy who figured out how to climb back up again.

After getting his ass kicked by life — and his own stupidity — for years, Murphy turned to writing as a way to share the lessons he's learned and the messy business of being a man today. His latest work, *Big Dick Energy: How to Be Well-Endowed (With Healthy Male Confidence)*, blends humor, raw honesty, and hard-earned wisdom to throw a grenade into the self-help genre.

When he's not writing, you'll probably find him kayaking, walking on the beach, drinking cheap beer, or singing karaoke at Central Florida dive bars. Shara's probably within arm's reach.

He's also forgetful when the dishwasher needs loaded, but he relies on his — as they've been described —"soft as a woman's" lips to keep himself out of the doghouse.

If you meet him, don't let his resting bitch face intimidate you. He's a decent enough guy.

Your Notes

www.ingramcontent.com/pod-product-compliance
Lightning Source LLC
Chambersburg PA
CBHW071519120626
46550CB00006B/2276